D0936478

ALDOUS HUXLEY
RECOLLECTED

Baskoody

Aldous Huxley
August 2nd
1962

ALDOUS HUXLEY RECOLLECTED
An Oral History

David King Dunaway

Carroll & Graf Publishers, Inc.
New York

Copyright © 1995 by David King Dunaway

All rights reserved.

First Carroll & Graf edition 1995

Carroll & Graf Publishers, Inc.
260 Fifth Avenue
New York, NY 10001

Library of Congress Cataloging-in-Publication Data is available.

Manufactured in the United States of America

PREFACE
"Aldous"
by
Francis Huxley

Aldous. How well the name suited him, and how often have I heard people refer to him with familiar reverence by that name alone, as though there were but one Aldous in the history of the world! They thus honored him as a novelist with a wittily scabrous eye for the grotesque and the pretentious; as an essayist who played variations of art, music, morals, hypnotism, and overpopulation, and who looked at ends and means, science, culture, religion, and society; as an anthologist of poetry or of the Perennial Philosophy; as a Utopist, a pacifist, a student of the Bates method, of the Alexander technique, of E therapy; as the herald of the psychedelic revolution, or as the patron saint of a New Age set on beleaguered Island, whose familiar spirit was a mynah bird calling Attention! Attention! Or, finally as one who, three days before he died, longingly remarked that one could write the greatest book ever written—if one knew how—"by bringing it all in."

"What are you thinking about, Aldous dear?" his mother, Julia, once asked him when he, aged four, was staring out the window into the garden. "Skin," he had replied.

His head was, of course, very large—so large that when he was learning to walk, it overbalanced him and caused

him to constantly topple. It certainly marked him out as an exceptional child whose character, everyone agreed, was quite out of the ordinary, and as he grew, to what became an exceptional height, he acquired a posture of body and mind that is best described as Aldousian, and that F. Matthias Alexander did his best to put to rights.

But before Aldous was "Aldous," he was equally distinguished by the name of Ogie, diminutive of Ogre. My father Julian, his eldest brother, remembers him as sitting quietly a good deal of the time, contemplating the strangeness of things and showing some innate superiority even at the age of five.

Aldous could never remember his childhood in any detail, even when hypnotized by Milton Erickson. No wonder, perhaps, if he was then as silent, inscrutable, ogreish, antagonistic, and rather green, as Enid Bagnold remembered him. Julian was a headstrong child, and while Trevenen, the second brother, bore the brunt of his youthful bullying, Aldous learnt to be unbullyable by putting on a cloak of invisibility and simply disappearing.

What a family, with what alarming forebears the three boys were continually admonished to live up to! One side was headed by [our grandfather] Thomas Henry Huxley, the pugnacious rationalist, materialist, and agnostic who was called both "Darwin's Bulldog" and "Pope Huxley"; the other by [our great-grandfather] Thomas Arnold of Rugby, who reformed the English public school system with large infusions of Christian certainties. The effect of this right-mindedness caused his son, Julia's father, to change from Protestant to Catholic and back again to Protestant—which lost him his livelihood every time—and to turn Julia herself away from doctrinaire opinions of any kind. A remarkable woman by every account, whose motto for Prior's Field, the girls' school she founded, was something she brought alive in all that she did: "We live by Admiration, Hope, and Love."

Julia died when Aldous was fourteen, leaving him a letter

in which she asked him not to be too critical of other people and to love much. It might have been easier for him to heed this advice had his father, Leonard, the son of Thomas Henry, not behaved more like a fellow schoolboy than a father. Aldous was fond of him, but thought him silly—silly enough, indeed, to be caricatured in his novels. Leonard was not, as Gervas Huxley remembered, the kind of father one looked up to, or went to when in trouble. Had he been, Trevenen would surely not have hanged himself when undergoing treatment for a severe nervous breakdown brought on both by having fallen in love with the chambermaid and having got only second class honours in his examination for the Civil Service.

Margaret, the youngest of the Huxley children, described Trevenen as the hub of the family wheel after Julia died. It is perhaps no wonder that this hub broke under the high and competing moral tones of the Huxley and Arnold strains within him. I do not know that Aldous, then more or less blind, had taken much notice of Trevenen's difficulties: Julian had already had two nervous breakdowns from which he had recovered, and Thomas Henry had had several in his later life. It was easy to regard this propensity as an inherited disorder, as Julian always did, whose cure was best left in the doctor's hands. All the same, I do wonder at Aldous's idea of becoming a doctor in the days when he still had his sight. Surely he was then well aware of what the skeletons in the family closet could set up to, and was looking for some kind of cure not only to their goings-on but to the human condition itself.

Meanwhile, his lack of natural piety was developing hand in hand with a kind of Pyrrhonian indifference into a classic example of the schizothymic temperament: as it was then being called. He drew consummate portraits of this unhappy state, in *Eyeless in Gaza* and *Point Counter Point* and later refined it in the light of Dr. Sheldon's typology, which made him out to be an ectomorph—tall, lanky, and with more skin in proportion to his weight than the muscular mesomorph or the rotund endomorph. Aldous was very pleased with this diagnosis, which he often remarked on: how could he be expected to write like, say, Balzac, whose guts—at least three times as long as his own—gave him such unparalleled stamina as a novelist, such ease in digesting the emotions?

By the time he was writing *Eyeless in Gaza* he had found three treatments for that difficulty: colonic irrigation, diet, and the Alexander technique. Before then, however, his ailment was still all in his head, and he heroically diagnosed himself by writing it out in *Point Counter Point*. With extraordinary courage he had focused his irreverent gaze on the forbidden places in himself and, as Isaiah Berlin remarked, had minutely and fully described "intimate physical experience, the faintest reference to which used to affect him with a feeling of violent guilt."

Aldous did not at all like Freud, principally because he ignored the neurological and biochemical level that so profoundly affects our lives. How can mental disorders stemming from these levels be treated by psychological means alone? he asked. He therefore did not depend on Freud when writing about Swift, whose odious and excrementitious obsessions left him fascinated and dismayed.

D. H. Lawrence had his own thoughts about *Point Counter Point*. "I have read it with a heart sinking through my boot-soles and a rising admiration" he wrote, going on to castigate Aldous for thrilling only to murder, suicide, and rape. Aldous's stepmother and other relatives were equally displeased with him for botanising on his mother's grave, and for using some of his father's more ludicrous and unhappy traits to flesh out one of the characters in the book. He was surprised by the hubbub, as surprised perhaps as he was when Lady Ottoline Morrell took exception to her portrait in *Crome Yellow:* and one could perhaps justify this surprise by remembering that he was, after all, an ectomorphic schizothyme who would never write like Balzac (and never, never like Proust).

I cannot imagine how he would have fared in this situation had it not been for Maria, his first wife.

"Insofar as I have learnt to be human—and I had a great capacity for not being human—it is thanks to her," he said. It was she who bridged the gap between his intellectual and physical time, if only by divining for him the nature of the present moment. As dragoman to this exceptionally intelligent tourist in the realms of feeling, she cleared his social way, laid bare the emotional bones of his friends and acquaintances, locked him in his study for his daily stint of writing, read aloud whatever difficult books he required for his work, and put him on diets. Then there was D. H. Lawrence, with whom he had a necessary and unlikely friendship, and who could give so much that it was a waste of time to argue with him concerning those matters—science, for example—about which he was fantastically unreasonable.

I wish I could have sat in on the conversations (I was four at the time) when Aldous and Maria, Lawrence and Frieda, came to Les Diablerets, on my parents' [Julian and Juliette Huxley] invitation. Aldous was still glued to *Point Counter Point*, Julian was in the throes of writing *The Science of Life* with H. G. Wells and his son Gip, and Lawrence had just finished *Lady Chatterley's Lover*—about which my mother has contradictory opinions. (She was then embroidering a picture of Adam and Eve, of her own design, to which Lawrence, expert needleman that he was, gave the finishing pubic touches.) Julian and Aldous had been reliving their childhoods by reading *The Pickwick Papers* aloud of an evening, before the Lawrences arrived; and then, I suppose, Lawrence broke up the happy home by swiping at Julian for being a professional scientist and Wordsworthian voyeur, at Aldous for being an intellectual-aesthetic pervert, and at the absent Wells for being a bigger interfering know-all than either of them. It must have been very invigorating.

Lawrence certainly talked about his little ranch in New Mexico, and perhaps also about Rananim, the quite un-Wellsian Utopian community he wanted Aldous to help

start. Aldous had been tempted. Communes and Utopias
were very much to his intellectual taste, though he would
have been sorely tried had he actually lived in one. He had,
after all, lived at Garsington, Bloomsbury's country house,
and found it wanting even when he did his war service there
as a conscientiously objecting farmhand. But he was now
well on the way to imagining his own anti-Wellsian Brave
New World in New Mexico, to take advantage of the Savages there. How Wells had hated him for that book. Trea-
son to science, he called it, and defeatist pessimism. But
that was some years before Wells confessed bankruptcy
in *Mind at the End of Its Tether*, by which time Aldous
was heading for the doomed Utopias of *After Many a
Summer* and *Island* via small-scale technology, decentral-
ized economy, hypnasogc education, yogic exercises, tan-
tric observances, and Soma, and where the only savages
in view were politicians and the representatives of international commerce.

I think the first real savages Aldous saw were on his visit
to Brazil, courtesy of that country's government. His visit
made a large stir in Rio, the papers being full of the opinions of O Sabio, the Sage. It was as though the Leaning
Tower of Pisa had come to town, he wrote. But a much
larger compliment was in store for him when he was then
flown into the Xingu reservation, which had been set up by
those three remarkable Indianists, the Villas Boas brothers.
Having visited the place myself, I can imagine Aldous fastid-
iously stepping along the path from the airstrip to the
agency buildings, dressed in a pale silk suit, with matching
shoes and panama hat, and surrounded by plump, delightful girls and a naked and admiring crowd of copper-
colored youth with well-oiled, stocky bodies, their hair
plastered with red urucu paint. He then had to introduce
himself to an unkempt and astonished Claudio, the intellectual of the three brothers, who had just returned from
a jungle trip. On being told that here was Aldous Huxley,
Claudio rapturously cried out, "Ooshley! Ooshley! Con-

trapunto!" and hugged him Brazilian fashion with tears streaming from his eyes.

I have never learnt what Aldous made of the remarkable tribes that lived on the reservation. Had they been devotees of the ayahuasca vine, Claudio might have arranged a hallu-cinogenic festival for Aldous to take part in, since his visit, after all, was some years after he had been introduced to mescaline. But this could not be. However, the image of O Sabio, somewhat frail and benignly self-contained as he overtops by at least a foot these brave and healthy inhabit-ants of an ancient world, offers a contrast that F. M. Alexan-der would have made much of. To be a large-headed, half-blind schizothymic ectomorph standing six foot four inches tall (on the few occasions that he wasn't folded up in a chair at his desk) is enough to turn a man into a giraffe, and to humanize this mythical beast with Alexandrian technique was a task that took him many years. One of its key exercises is to imagine, as you walk, that you are suspended by a hair from the very crown of your head, which gives you your vertical. It did seem to me, however, that Aldous would lean over backwards to follow this precept, by tucking in his chin and walking as though carrying the Tower of Pisa on his head. But what Alexander could not entirely rectify, try as he might, Humphry Osmond did without giving the matter a thought. For it was Osmond who launched Aldous on his first mescaline adventure, who (with Maria) sat with him while vision flooded his being, who put him into a car to visit the World's Biggest Drugstore and the hills above Los Angeles. And there Osmond took a photograph of him as he looked, eyeless no longer, over the unmeaning distances of this modern Gaza. Though but a snap, it immortalizes Aldous Redivivus as he stands solid, upright, buoyant, with his chin in the position that nature intended, demonstrating what happens when the doors of perception are not only cleansed but properly hung . . .

That Aldous missed this fundamental shift in his postural economy when he came to write about his experience is not surprising. Though he had wonderfully improved his imaginative sight by means of the Bates method—and what a remarkable faculty that was from the beginning, which (as Kenneth Clark remarked) made this nearly blind man one of the most discerning lookers at paintings and architecture of our time—it was only with mescaline that this could be effortlessly married to the realities of outer light. "This is how one ought to see," he kept exclaiming, and later: "Anyone who has ever had the experience of seeing the world without any labels and concepts, immediately has the impression of its being supernatural."

No wonder then that his astonishment and gratitude were expressed as praise of the beatific vision he had glimpsed, a form of words for which he was rated by theologically minded critics. No wonder, too, that his delight in the vibrant profundities of this newborn sense made him turn his eyes away from Osmond and even Maria, whose complicated humanity could only disturb the Not-Self he had miraculously become.

For this failure to engage in the I-Thou relationship he was roundly castigated by Martin Buber, some years after the event. But Aldous was not the man to gloss over his own faults, and when he next took mescaline he remembered what his mother had written him on her death-bed: "Don't be too critical of other people," and "love much." This advice he did his best to follow in his remaining years (as Laura, his second wife, happily attested to) in spite of tragedies to come of which I need not speak, in spite of those difficulties in personal communication that, he supposed, he would never entirely get rid of. In spite of pain, death, and horror, he saw that the universe was fundamentally All Right, capital A, capital R.

Is this not the message that he would like us all to listen to in these parlous days: love much, and bring it all in?

"For practical purposes one tries to make a little scientific and ethical sense of it all; for non-practi-

cal purposes—aesthetic and 'spiritual'—one cultivates Wordsworth's 'wise passiveness' and opens oneself receptively to the MYSTERIUM TREMENDUM ET FASCINANS within and without.

Ever your affectionate

Aldous"

Santa Fe, New Mexico   April 1992

CONTENTS

INTRODUCTION

A decade ago, I began writing a biography of
Aldous Huxley (1894–1963), whom the *Paris
Review* considered "one of the most prodi-
giously learned writers not merely of our century but
of all time."[1]
The most surprising discovery of my research was how many
critics dismissed virtually everything Huxley wrote from
midlife on, after he had moved to the United States. The
man whose *Brave New World* was translated into twenty-
eight languages is presumed to have dulled his literary edge
under the California sun. Known primarily for his biting
satires of Britain's literary set in the years after World War I—
including H. G. Wells, T. S. Eliot, and Virginia Woolf—few
realized that Huxley's life had a second act in America, in
Hollywood's Golden Age. There he worked on films alongside F. Scott Fitzgerald (who profiled him in *The Last Tycoon* as "Boxley"), Christopher Isherwood, and Igor
Stravinsky; and in his quarter-century in the U.S., he wrote
nineteen books. In Los Angeles, he mingled with the glitter-
ing European emigrant community of the 1940s, including
Thomas and Heinrich Mann, Bertolt Brecht, Charles
Chaplin, and Greta Garbo.

Yet Huxley's work in Hollywood studios (on such films as
Jane Eyre and *Pride and Prejudice*) was considered inconse-
quential or voyeuristic; his study of Indian religions was de-
rided as so much "yogi-bogey."[2] After months of such
diatribes in the domed reading room of the British Museum,
I shifted my goal to writing not a life but a half-life; to apply
interdisciplinary training in American Studies to Huxley's
American years, 1937–1963, which literary historians characterized so dourly.

The more one reads Aldous Huxley's critics, the more one finds divided opinions of which Huxley they favor: the early poet, under the influence of Stéphane Mallarmé and other symbolist poets; the young skeptic, whose novels were as important to the between-the-wars generation as Bob Dylan was to those growing up in the 1960s; the august and mordant essayist, in the Matthew Arnold tradition; the religious stylite who spent World War II compiling texts on the common (mystical) ground of the world's religions; or "the gentle guru of Beverly Hills," as one critic characterized those attracted to Huxley as a psychedelic pioneer and proto-hippie.[3]

Although writers as thoughtful as Margaret Drabble in the 1989 *Oxford Companion to English Literature* continue to disregard his American years, these years represented not a loss of his powers so much as the forging of a new personality—and persona. Huxley became obsessed with enlightenment in its physical and spiritual senses. He shed the mantle of prize cynic for the vocation of a social educator, seeking a refined human psychology. "Huxley saw foolish consistency as the hobgoblin of little minds ..." one prominent Huxley scholar has written.

"The sense of Huxley's method is that it finds theology too doctrinaire, philosophy too abstract, literature too formalistic, and life, complex life, greatly to be cared about, marvelled at and deplored, all at once."[4]

Over one hundred books have been written on Aldous Huxley (including dissertations), yet only six could be called biographical. The principal reason for this imbalance is a flash fire in the Hollywood Hills in 1961, which destroyed Huxley's papers: letters, manuscripts of D. H. Lawrence, annotations to his enormous library. His letters survive—occasionally on his writing, although he discussed works-in-progress only in sketchy terms—and more than three thousand of his wife's letters to her family, written in French, in the Belgian Royal Library. This work poses crucial, unanswered questions about Huxley's American sojourn. Were the writings of the American years as self-indulgent as critics claimed? What sort of a screenwriter was he; did this nearly blind writer ever learn the craft? What was his role in the studios? How and why did he become involved with mysticism and vision-inducing drugs? Did he ever reach that unitary experience he sought throughout the last decades of his life?

This is a book of responses to these and other queries—from the witnesses, co-workers, family, and friends of Aldous Huxley. The two dozen interviewees included here range from movie stars to private citizens—accounts of people who hiked with Huxley, signed his contracts, breakfasted with him, or obtained books for him. Included are people who drove him across the country and those who cooked his Sunday roast. The youngest person interviewed was thirty and the oldest ninety-eight (Aldous Huxley's stepmother).[5]

Those included are, by literary intent, a community—although many have never spoken or crossed paths with one another. Several are prominent in their own professions: as documentary filmmakers, scholars, psychologists, and librarians. Some are distinguished authors, such as Lady Naomi Mitchison and Christopher Isherwood. About the only characteristic the narrators share is their concern for Aldous Leonard Huxley, whom they have agreed to memorialize. Of course the majority of those alive today can testify only to Huxley's post-emigration period in the U.S. thus any volume built on oral testimony must concentrate disproportionately on this period.

This imbalance of sources is only one reason why literary history built upon reminiscence often cannot resolve scholarly debates, particularly ones as partisan as the value of Aldous Huxley's American writings. Though oral biographies of contemporary writers Norman Mailer or Jack Kerouac have made major contributions to the scholarship on these authors, their primary focus is inevitably on the man's life, rather than the work.[6] The contributors to this volume are not primarily critics or literary historians so much as witnesses to Huxley's development as an author and a man.

At a symposium on Huxley's work in the *London Magazine* in 1955, nothing the author wrote after 1939 was discussed seriously: his later novels were dismissed as "largely indigestible"; his essays written in the U.S. were mentioned not at all.[7] The chasm separating Huxley's British and American careers became most acute during World War II (when for the first time, his books appeared first in American editions); but the reader awaiting a definitive answer on which period was superior may not find satisfaction in these pages, for collections of oral history rarely argue a single thesis. With its overlapping, and at times contradictory, reports, oral history meanders on its way to truth, accreting evidence from its interviewees.

The ethnography of an interview is its situation and its interaction, yet conveying the multiple contexts of these interviews is difficult. We spoke in lofty mansions in the Hollywood Hills and in ordinary subdivisions in the San Fernando Valley north of Los Angeles. The smell of jasmine and surf drifted up from one cabana in Malibu, the street noise and soot of inner-city Los Angeles are imprinted on the recording of another. On occasion, I began interviews informally over coffee, with the rattle of porcelain forever overlaid on the tape; sometimes I sat up stiffly in offices where phones rang continually and assistants hovered.

My interviews with Huxley's widow, Laura Archera Huxley, were conducted in the house in the Hollywood Hills where Aldous Huxley died, below a tall window flooding the room with sunlight, which was further reflected by a bone-white carpet. In London, I spoke with Lady Juliette, widow of Julian Huxley, the first director general of UNESCO, in a second-floor library in Belsize Park, as a portrait of Sir Julian glowered down upon us.

My interview with the eldest sister of Maria Huxley (Aldous Huxley's first wife) took place in the salon of her darkly lit Paris apartment; there she entrusted to me letters written by her daughter, Sophie, who lived with the Huxleys in Hollywood. I talked with a beekeeper north of Los Angeles, in the windy desert outpost where the Huxleys lived during World War II; he remembered Huxley as an erect and tall Englishman poised cross-legged in a field, staring toward the desert horizon.

Although this volume is designed to be read on its own, as literary history of a notable member of Hollywood's most literary period, it may serve as a companion volume to my demi-biography, *Huxley in Hollywood*. Some readers might wonder why that book does not contain passages included in this one. Similarly, statements in this work occasionally challenge assumptions or assertions in the earlier volume. Confronting such contradictions, I have reflected on how the evidentiary value of a fact is linked to its provenance. Sometimes the best stories are "set pieces," or rehearsed anecdotes of the past. Even where unauthenticatable—as is much orally collected information—these narratives may stand as literary-historical texts on their own. Appreciating them does not compel one to believe them.

Of the nearly one hundred interviews I conducted from June 1985 to June 1990, not all were recorded, nor has everyone interviewed agreed to inclusion in this volume.

This book could have numbered nine hundred pages, for less than a tenth of the material here has ever been published. But that length would not have served the purpose of this volume: not a definitive study as much as an intimate avenue into one of the most influential British novelists of this century—an author whose style and approach bridge the late Victorian era (in which he was raised) and the present day. This volume might introduce an author whose sixty books are not always accessible, in his time and in ours, and whose cultural context—particularly for the American years—has sometimes been misread.

From these pages a portrait of Huxley emerges that may challenge the traditional image of the author as "a moun-

tainously remote, icy intellectual," as Isherwood puts it in
these pages: the revered but cynical, smart-set novelist of
the 1920s.[8] To appreciate Huxley's work as a whole, and
particularly the later work, we need to understand the preoccupations documented here: his preoccupation with overcoming his physical handicap and seeing, visually and
metaphorically; and his realization that our potential for self-
knowledge as a species has barely been tapped.

The most lengthy of these interviews, one-third of the
total number, were tape-recorded, transcribed, and re-
viewed by the narrators, who often corrected their transcripts for dates and/or spellings; in seven cases,
interviewees sealed transcripts (or passages) referring to individuals in Huxley's life. In the next decades, when these
seals are removed, few literary nuggets will be revealed,
although rivalries within his circle will become clear. (Complete, transcripts are available to scholars at the Huntington
Library in San Marino, California.)

Transcribing and editing oral history are procedures fairly
well agreed upon within the field, yet the edited excerpts
which follow are by no means methodologically transparent.
One of the dangerous conceits of popular autobiography is
the omission of how spoken words become a carefully arranged text. (An appendix describes how this volume was
assembled, together with a methodological essay on transcribing and oral literary history.)

The first five chapters examine Huxley's life in chronological order; editorial interpolations are marked with brackets.
These chapters, interleaved by an abbreviated narrative,
are followed by responses of critics to Huxley's legacy
and contemporary reception; a checklist of Huxley's major
publications and residences; and a note on those
interviewed.

My hope is that readers will be inspired to read more
of Aldous Huxley, and to find among these recollections
a complicated but congenial figure, a writer whose work

profoundly moved at least two generations of readers in this century.

London, England
Albuquerque, New Mexico
January 1994

ALDOUS HUXLEY
RECOLLECTED

Chapter I
England: Family, Youth, Parenthood
(1894–1936)

Reducing the complexities of a life to a few pages is unsatisfying to the specialist; it is like drafting a comic-book version of an opera without music or acting. Yet the reader may want a brief biographical overview before reading the accounts that follow.[1]

Aldous Leonard Huxley was born in the county of Surrey, England, in 1894 to a family of scientists, educators, and critics. He was the grandson of Thomas Henry Huxley (1825–1895), biologist science writer, and lecturer—the man often called ''Darwin's bulldog'' for mustering data and publicly supporting Charles Darwin's then-controversial theories of evolution. Aldous Huxley's great-uncle on his mother's side was Matthew Arnold, the nineteenth-century poet and essayist whose writing exemplifies the romantic pessimism of an age torn between the promises of science and religion. Many writers have commented on the significance of Huxley's birth at the confluence of two of Britain's prominent families in science and letters.[2]

The Huxley household was overshadowed by Grandpater, as T. H. was called. Leonard Huxley (1860–1933), Aldous's fa-

ther, eventually devoted five years to a two-volume biography
of T. H. Leonard was a head teacher who wrote a number of
biographies and edited the literary *Cornhill Magazine*. Aldous's
mother, Julia Arnold, was a schoolmistress. The three sons (Julian, Trevenen, and Aldous) were significantly separated in age
from their sister Margaret (eight years younger than Aldous).
Margaret, who converted to the Church of England, migrated to
South Africa, and eventually became a schoolmistress in Kent,
is in many ways the missing person (and perhaps the greatest
rebel) of the Huxley saga. She apparently had little contact and
correspondence with her brothers.

Educated in keeping with family tradition at Eton and Balliol College, Oxford, as were his two older brothers, Julian,
the world-famous biologist, and Trevenen, Aldous embarked
on a fast track to literary success. Gravitating toward his
father's occupations, he worked briefly as a teacher at Eton,
where his students included Eric Blair (George Orwell), then
moved to London as a literary journalist for the *Athenaeum*,
Vanity Fair, and *Vogue*. His first volumes of poetry were
praised by Marcel Proust. About his first novel, *Crome Yellow*
(1921), F. Scott Fitzgerald wrote, "This is the highest point
so far obtained by Anglo-Saxon sophistication. Huxley is the
wittiest man now writing in English."[3] The author so lauded
was not yet thirty.

In the next decade, Huxley's novels epitomized the disaffection of the generation that had survived World War I.
Works like *Point Counter Point* (1928) and *Brave New World*
(1932)—as well as a half-dozen well-received collections of
essays—established Huxley's worldwide reputation as a satirist. The author lived in Italy and France, processing his reading and travels into two and three books per year. By the age
of forty, he had been translated into two dozen languages.
His fame rivaled that of his literary friends Virginia Woolf,
T. S. Eliot, H. G. Wells, and D. H. Lawrence.

The engine fueling Huxley's well-known satire was a life
framed by personal tragedies that occurred during his adoles-

cence. At fourteen, his mother died suddenly of cancer. A year and a half later, Huxley was stricken by a streptococcal infection in his eyes, leaving him completely blind for a year—and then permanently disabled, with visual capacity in only a quarter of one eye. When Aldous was twenty, his brother Trevenen committed suicide, a victim of an inherited family tendency to chronic depression—a syndrome that later plagued his second brother, Julian. Despite these setbacks, the tall, fragile-boned intellectual with columnar body and oversize head, finished his Oxford degree with first-class honors, and eventually wrote some sixty books.[4]

In 1936, following the publication of *Eyeless in Gaza* and a paralyzing writer's block, Huxley's writing changed from a sardonic tone to being "explicitly serious in intention . . . with an increasing interest in pacifism and Indian religion."[5] After the outbreak in 1936 of the Civil War in Spain, when many radicals changed their political philosophy from pacifism to collective security against Nazism, Huxley was reviled by his former associates for retaining an absolutist opposition to war. Cecil Day Lewis called him "the Prophet of Disgust." Stephen Spender attacked *Eyeless in Gaza* as a work continuing much muddled thinking: "We had to wait for Aldous Huxley to propose that prayers are an exercise for the soul, like an elastic exerciser or a dose of Eno's Fruit Salts."[6]

In the company of his friend Gerald Heard, a science commentator for the British Broadcasting Corporation, Huxley moved his family to the United States in 1937, a watershed event. He would live there for the rest of his years, first in New Mexico on D. H. Lawrence's ranch, then in Los Angeles and its environs. Although Huxley came to the United States to lecture on pacifism, he ended up working at Metro-Goldwyn-Mayer, Twentieth Century-Fox, and other studios, authoring screenplays with other émigrés such as Zoltan Korda and Christopher Isherwood. His American period was characterized by a dramatic shift in his writing, from the cynicism of his post-World War I generation to an ardent exploration of mysticism, parapsychology, and Indian religions.

From the 1932 publication of *Brave New World* onward, Huxley wrote in a prophetic and apocalyptic mode. In that year, he predicted genetic engineering; in 1944, he warned of the dangers of nuclear energy; in 1947, of environmental catastrophes. Huxley became a twentieth-century Tiresias, a blind seer whose predictions were accurate but unwelcomed.

Few alive today recall the young Aldous Huxley. The accounts that follow are from these few individuals, supplemented by anecdotes of his early years from close friends and family, including the two sisters of Maria Nys, Huxley's first wife, whom he married in 1919.

In these recollections, Aldous Huxley appears by turns ambitious, melancholy, and courageous as he undertook to finish his education despite the sudden deaths of his brother and mother, and his childhood blindness. His is a literary success story, as the urbane collegian takes his first steps toward world renown.

We begin with Juliette Huxley, widow of Aldous's elder brother Julian, recalling the challenges of Aldous's youth and his university days.

Juliette Huxley (sister-in-law)

Leonard was the son of [the eminent biologist] T. H. Huxley. T. H. was a great person in the family and so they [Leonard and Julia's boys: Julian, Trev, and Aldous] had to be worthy of him. Now Julian suffered from that. Very much. The middle brother, Trevenen, you could say he died by his own hand [August 23, 1914] because of that pressure. There were other reasons at the time; he didn't get a First [class Honors degree at Balliol College, Oxford]; he didn't get a job at the Foreign Office where he had applied—well, there were three hundred or so applicants, and about six got in. What I heard of [Trev] really puts him as a very great person.

Their mother, Julia Arnold, was the niece of Matthew Arnold, whose grandfather was Thomas Arnold of Rugby [a prominent nineteenth-century English educator]—again, a

kind of ancestral dominance. She was a brilliant education-
ist. She founded the school at Prior's Field near Godalming,
Surrey [opened January 23, 1902]. The four children were
born there, at Prior's Field. Leonard Huxley, Julian's father,
was a very kind, very lovely person. But he didn't have
that—whatever you call it. He brought up his family, and
he was a teacher at Charterhouse. He never pierced into
being world famous, except that he published his father's
Life and Letters (a wonderful, absolutely marvelous piece
of work) and *Jane Welsh Carlyle* [and several other books].
He did very good work, but you wouldn't call it really outstanding, the way his father's was. He brought his children
up to be worthy of their grandfather.

Julia Arnold Huxley died [November 29, 1908] when [Al-
dous was fourteen and] Margaret was six years old. The
child was left, adoring her mother, in the school with a
partner of her mother, a Mrs. Burton-Brown, who then took
over the direction of the school. Mrs. Burton-Brown could
have been said to be rather brutal to Margaret; she was a
little child, coming from the other side of the school. Margaret then was sent to various relations because her father
couldn't cope with a child of six, naturally.

Leonard married again [on February 23, 1912]; his second wife was a Scottish lady called Rosalind Bruce. She
landed in the nest of eagles. There was Julian; there was
Trevenen; there was Aldous; there was little Margaret, who
was not happy. She couldn't possibly give her loyalty and
her love to somebody else so very different from her
mother. Somehow she became separate from the family.
She didn't get on with her stepmother. Margaret became a
Christian, and, of course, Leonard was an agnostic. And
people who are firmly agnostic are just as intolerant reli-
giously as the old missionaries, and so forth.

Margaret said to Francis once: "When Trev died, it was
as if a bomb had exploded in the family. It got separated."
Julian went his way, Aldous went his way, and Margaret
went hers.

Laura Huxley (second wife)

In the chapter of Aldous's autobiography (in my book, *This Timeless Moment*) he speaks about his grandfather and himself as a child, and I think he mentions that he as a child couldn't possibly imagine what his grandfather was undergoing—why this pain, why the discomfort was in his body. He spoke about the two different worlds of his grandfather and himself.

In his two-volume autobiography *Memories*, Julian Huxley wrote that his father, Leonard, was not "a typical Huxley, nor was his brother Harry, the surgeon. It seems as if the Huxley genes skipped a generation to assert their particular characteristics, which are perhaps best defined as temperamental, in his grandchildren."[7] The mother, Julia Arnold, was the pivot of the family, organizing picnic lunches for the boys in the Surrey countryside and reading to them in the early evenings—a penchant for literature read aloud that Aldous Huxley cherished all his life, especially after his childhood blinding.

Julian recounts the day he read his mother's journal for the first time, as she lay dying of cancer in November 1908: " 'My dear, dear son. You have brought me only joy since you were laid in my arms, a little downy bundle, that June day in 1887. It is very hard to leave you all—but after these weeks of quiet thought, I know that life is but one—and that I am only going into another room of the sounding labor-house vast of Being . . .' My mother was buried . . . Trev and I were on the verge of tears, and Aldous, then at the critical age of fourteen, stood in stony misery. We know now, from several of his early novels, what sense of irreparable bereavement occupied his mind and soul; I am sure that this meaningless catastrophe was the main cause of the protective cynical skin in which he clothed himself and his novels in the twenties."[8]

Of the traumatic shocks of his youth, none would become such a burden (or inspiration) to Huxley as the challenge of overcoming his blindness. The most complete account of this episode is from his sister-in-law Juliette Huxley's memoir, *Leaves of the Tulip Tree:*

His uncle Henry Huxley visited Aldous in Eton—accidentally, on a Sunday, as he was coming back from a visit in the country. Harry Huxley was a surgeon and he found Aldous with an enormous compress on a very badly inflamed eye. He called the matron, Gertrude Ward. She didn't really know anything about health. Harry Huxley said, 'My God!' And the matron said, 'It's a stye.' Harry said , 'No. It's much more serious. I'm taking him straightaway to London.'

He brought him to a specialist in London [at the Institute, now School, of Tropical Medicine] who declared this boy had keratitis in the eye. The one eye was gone—finished, ruined. He was going to try and save the other. So, for nearly two years, Aldous walked about with a bandage across his eyes, unable to use his eyes because they had to rest. He was parked from one cousin to another, one aunt to another. [Novelist] Mrs. Humphrey Ward was his aunt. She looked after him quite a while. He had a very good tutor who was himself a young student at Oxford. He became Sir George Clark, Emeritus Professor of History. He taught Aldous [enough] to get through to his Balliol scholarship, which he won."[9]

His blindness was one of the few parts of his personal life about which Aldous Huxley would write and talk: here friends report on what they heard and observed of Huxley's physical vision.

Peggy Kiskadden (friend)

He told me once that at spring vacation [1910] with his aunt and uncle, they played this card game. At the beginning of the vacation, he played it. At the end of the vacation, he couldn't decipher the cards. It came so suddenly, the keratitis [a streptococcus infection]. He had planned to be a doctor. He was frustrated—he had the Huxley interest in science, and I think he had his mother's concern for people.

She must've been a lovely person, and the combination made him want very much to be a doctor.

He might've gone into research, but he had a care for people, he really had, and it made him very bitter, and I think that bitterness is so clear in the early books.

Naomi Haldane Mitchison (friend)

We were both from scientific families and we thought that what grown-ups do was to go into science. That was the main thing. Anything else was less reliable.

I think he had a pretty miserable time when he went blind. His father didn't really take it seriously enough. He was at Eton, and somehow or another, people helped him a lot. When he came to Oxford, it was really quite impossible for him to go to college. But he wanted to start his degree. So he came to stay with us. That was [around] 1914. He and the war came together.

His father just didn't seem to bother very much. I'd known them; my parents were very angry with his father for not doing more [about his eye disease, *Keratitis punctata*] and [not] believing him. Remember, in those days medicine was rather different, and they weren't very good at finding out exactly what was wrong.

My parents helped him a lot, but he didn't talk to me about his blindness. We just talked. You don't really talk about that sort of thing to a fifteen-year-old schoolgirl.

He was very brave; he wouldn't complain of anything. He was really rather proud of managing to learn braille music. He was extremely intelligent about how he dealt with his blindness. You didn't think of him as a blind person—at least I didn't.

Later in his life he was always trying things out which might help. He would have liked to be able to see properly. He was very much more blind when he was staying with us than he was even five years afterwards. He'd got slightly better—enough for him to get about. But when he first came to us, he was almost totally blind.

I remember him walking up the stairs just with four fingers on the bannister. The walking was going quite fast.

Although he looked blind, he wasn't quite blind. You treated him very gently. He was tall and stooping when I met him. He moved rather slowly, using his hands.

He and Julian both blamed their father very much for the death when Trev killed himself. They certainly felt that it was something that shouldn't have happened. I was very, very upset because I was very fond of Trev. It probably helped them a little to comfort me a bit.

Juliette Huxley (sister-in-law)

His eyes always gave trouble. At times, the one-quarter of one eye which Aldous had left became strained. You see, he tried to paint—when he was at [his house in southern France] Sanary, for instance—on the good, lovely days. He loved painting, but he found it took so much energy from his one eye that he had to give it up. He had to earn a living by typing, writing, and reading.

Julian had nervous breakdowns—maybe inherited from the grandfather. As you know, the grandfather had these bouts of what he called "black melancholy." Julian had two breakdowns before he was married—before I knew him—and five after we were married.

Now Aldous's breakdowns were not that sort, but I don't know how you describe them. I know he had more than one; I think Maria [Nys Huxley, Aldous's first wife] had some very difficult times with him. You see, these Huxleys were fragile people. Genius is a fragile quality. And if it's strained to a point where it doesn't seem to give the kind of reward, or the kind of enlightenment, something cracks.

There was something really devastating about having a grandfather (grandpater as they called him) who was a god in the family. These children grow up with that atmosphere: "Worthy of grandpater—right! You must be worthy of grandpater." It's a Greek story, isn't it?

Julian was rather ebullient as compared to Aldous, who

was not. Aldous was meditating, or he was listening, or he would suddenly say something very profound and very brilliant. Julian was sometimes telling funny stories which everybody enjoyed and laughed at. He was more of a releaser of intellectual heaviness.

Julian was the elder brother—six and a half years older. There was a big difference. Julian always was rather protective, because Aldous was a little brother and had been so often ill.

Aldous had a great admiration for his elder brother Julian who came home with all the prizes. He was a scholar of Balliol (College)—Brackenbury scholarship. He got a First in Zoology. Julian brought home the prizes. And, of course, the family expected him [Aldous] to. This was a burden that they put on their children.

Francis Huxley (nephew son of Julian Huxley)

Julia [Arnold] died when Julian was in his late teens, and Aldous was in his middle teens. It was a very bad moment for everyone. I think Margaret just got left out. Trevenen had the worst time, in a sense, because he fell in love with one of the chambermaids at the house, and he also got a Second at Oxford and a poor Civil Service examination. The combination of these matters gave him such a bad conscience that he killed himself. I think that's partly due to the fact that his mother was gone and his stepmother—as far as she could—tried to take care of this indigestible brood of young Huxleys. Leonard, after all (who was satirized by Aldous in one of his early novels), was not up to the mark either. It was he and his wife, Julia, who had, as far as I could see, instilled in them the necessity of being large brains, *grands cerveaux*, in the style of T. H. Huxley.

Margaret made the famous remark when she was at Oxford where she was a hockey-playing girl: "I have two brothers; one is an atheist and the other is interested in pleasure." She never said which was which.

Margaret became a schoolmistress. Her expectations of

following her mother and her father at Prior's Field—the family school—were cheated when [Margaret's] stepmother had given up her share of it to Mrs. Burton-Brown. She was very disappointed indeed. Then she started her own school. She had a female companion—a friend who died only a few years before her death. She wasn't in that category of high-powered intelligence at all. She was a very worthy educated woman. I've never heard a word from Aldous about her at all. My father never talked about her.

Aldous and Julian paralleled each other in an inverse manner; they were both mysterious to each other in some fashion. They got on with what they were best at. They had science and humanism as their bridges, and they used to make little forays to visit each other over these bridges.

Aldous was protected from the major weight of Julian's impatience by Trevenen. They grew up parallel, but [were] separated by Trevenen.

I never saw them [Julian and Aldous] being particularly chummy or affectionate in the sense that my brother and I are. It may be because they actually shared some large moments of intellectual discourse, and were fraternal in that region. I can't see them sharing confidentialities about each other's love lives or spiritual moments in any great way.

I think they'd chosen their own spheres of influence with great care. It had fallen out that their interests were in parallel, but not co-terminate; they didn't have to be competitive about it.

When Julian was in a—let us call it a "brown study"— the atmospheric mood around him did indeed go into brown, with touches of purple—kind of leatherish purple. When Aldous was in a mood, he would go into the bilious phase of that; he would go greenish. He absented himself from the conversation quite a lot. He would sit on the outskirts of conversation until he found that he was well placed to drop one of his long-playing records upon his turntable. Then he would perk up remarkably. Julian was a manic-depressive by temperament. Aldous I don't think was a manic-depressive; he was a melancholic in many ways. That's not a good enough description of him; he preferred [biologist] Dr. Sheldon's classification. He was an ectomorph.

Aldous Huxley's days at Balliol College, Oxford, were trying times. Most of his classmates were soldiers at the front and likely to return dead or wounded. Lady Naomi Mitchison remarked, "We were only so happy, when somebody came back with a wound, as my brother did, and got out."

With the help of his elder brothers, and particularly with the intellectual stimulation provided by Phillip and Ottoline Morrell at their estate near Oxford, Garsington, Aldous had the good fortune to be introduced to leading artistic and literary figures of his time. It was here that he knew Lytton Strachey, the distinguished biographer of his generation, T. S. Eliot, Bertrand Russell, and other major figures in the literary movement named after Bloomsbury, and the London district where Lady Ottoline had her townhouse.

Huxley began visiting the literary salon that was Garsington while still an undergraduate; he returned there for his alternative military service during the time when Russell and other pacifists were fixtures at the estate (and while Russell was having an affair with Ottoline). There Aldous and Julian both met their wives, causing the great hostess to murmur once that she was running a matrimonial bureau for the Huxleys. According to her biographer, Lady Ottoline considered Aldous's friendship with Maria to be ill-starred for a number of reasons. "He's so intellectual and so highly cultivated and self-absorbed; she so very passive and yet like all foreign girls, expecting so much attention."[10]

The connection that Aldous Huxley made with Maria Nys, nevertheless, became perhaps the most important human bond of his life; they were to be married for forty-four years, until her death. Although their sexual and domestic arrangements were unorthodox, Maria became not only his social secretary and manuscript typist, but also his "seeing-hearing eye dog," in the words of their only child, Matthew Huxley.[11]

Juliette Huxley (sister-in-law)

Aldous was at Balliol College [Oxford, October 1913–June 1914; December 1915–January 1916] still a student, working for his finals. He used to come for Sunday lunch or even [on] weekends from Oxford. I was teaching French to Julian Morrell, daughter of Lady Ottoline Morrell, at Garsington; she was a hostess who got together a lot of very interesting people—which, of course, interested Aldous enormously. He loved getting into that milieu. I got to know Aldous pretty well. And there was Maria, a refugee from Belgium— the Germans had come and invaded St. Trond where they lived; the mother [Marguerite] with four daughters [Maria's sisters: Suzanne, Rose, and Jeanne] had come to England. A cousin, the painter George Balthus, asked Lady Ottoline to take Maria as a refugee at the very beginning of the war, just after Belgium fell.

After a time, we noticed that Aldous was very much interested in Maria, who was incredibly beautiful. She had large, beautiful eyes—I think they were rather the color of her Egyptian scarab (which I think Aldous had given her), which was green-blue, a little gray in it—but her eyes were an extraordinary color and large. She had an oval face, a small chin, and very full lips—and a slightly aquiline nose.

Maria was really quite lovely, rather plump—puppy fat, I think you call it, a little distressed about it. And very silent. She hardly ever spoke. Nor did I, for that matter. Because there we were, in the middle of these highly intellectual people who discussed everything. It was an absolutely incredible milieu.

Aldous finished his finals [first-class at Oxford, 1916], although he was blind in one eye: an enormous achievement. He came to Garsington because he couldn't fight. He was not suitable for the Army. He was rejected—a C-3 [visual-physical disability, January 1916]. He had to go before a medical board, which rejected him completely. At one time, he rather wanted to join his friends. There was Lewis Gielgud [brother of the actor Sir John], a school friend who remained a friend all of his life. He was in the Army. There was Gervas Huxley, Aldous's favorite cousin—also in the Army. I think both were captains. Aldous was very keen to join them. But he simply couldn't do it.

So he came to Garsington, and the chance these men had during the war to help the war effort was to work on the land. That means cutting trees, or milking cows, or whatever. Some of them were called "conscientious objectors" because they did not want to have anything to do with the war.

There was a man called Gerald Shove, a conscientious objector and philosopher from Cambridge: a brilliant man, who hated the war very much. They were told "Cut this tree," or "Chop it up." So they came in their jodhpurs and their woolen stockings, hard after their jobs. There was also a stretcher-bearer, but not living at Garsington [David Garnett]; Duncan Grant, a painter, and Lytton Strachey and Mark Gertler.

People talked about painting and about Impressionists, about their last book and about Bertrand Russell (who, incidentally, was also there quite a long time). He also was against the war, of course, and he was put into prison for that.

Naomi Mitchison (friend)

Aldous came to Oxford in the war years. To some extent, we were all thinking about our brothers and friends being killed in France. We both thought about war a great deal. On the other hand, we were beginning to dabble in politics, and we started a cooperative shop. We all took turns to stand behind the counter, including Aldous and me. There were a lot of young poets going about, and it was a very odd time. You didn't know what was happening at all in that war. In all wars, an awful lot is hidden [by] people who are actually at the top, but most of all in that war. There were times when the people we were fond of came back wounded. But it was nice that Aldous was there. He was the one friend who I could always count on to be there—because he couldn't go out and be killed.

He was one of the people who acted in the two plays I wrote when I was quite young. He really quite enjoyed it.

We both knew several people who were straight pacifists. On the other hand, my brother was in France, and so were probably most of our friends.

Aldous's term at Garsington was [during] the war. I was never around to go to Garsington, though Aldous wanted me to come. I was still living with my parents, and they were quite strict.

The thing I remember most about Aldous during this time was [sitting] in the half-dark, talking. I had gotten engaged to be married in a year. He kept saying, "Tell me what it's like being in love. Are you in love?" I said, "I don't know. What really matters to me is that he doesn't get killed."

At the beginning of World War I, when Aldous Huxley met his first wife at the Morrells', he was a colorful character. Juliette remembers him striding down Oxford High Street in straw-colored jodhpurs and pale stockings with a dark-brown jacket, "absent-mindedly but absurdly romantic and beautiful. Even in those early days, he often seemed to be living in a remote and secret world, yet a word could spark off a brilliant discussion, revealing his astonishing erudition and memory. He also enjoyed the occasional malicious gossip of Bloomsbury visitors. He was, even among his close friends, the onlooker, the Jesting Pilate, relishing human foibles and suspecting the heroic."[12]

Both Juliette and Maria loved Lady Ottoline, but in different ways. Maria, though younger than Juliette, was more worldly; her crush on Ottoline led her at one point to threaten suicide when asked to leave the household, according to one of D. H. Lawrence's letters.[13]

Huxley's youth occurred during the flush days of the Bloomsbury group, when sexuality was very much on the agenda of his writer friends. As Virginia Woolf said, "Sex permeated our conversation. . . . We discussed copulation with the same excitement and openness that we had discussed the nature of good."[14] In the circle to which Aldous and Maria were drawn upon leaving Oxford, examples of homosexuality and bisexuality abounded: the Nicholsons, the Bells, Nancy Cunard, the Stracheys, and the Sitwells.

Rose D'Haulleville (sister-in-law Maria's younger sister)

Let me tell you: Maria was lesbian. What I've heard: when Maria was with Lady Ottoline, she was very much in love with her and had admiration for Lady Ottoline, who was, of course, a grand lady. She was very extraordinary with a big nose and fantastic clothes. [She] impressed Maria very much all her life. Maria had been raised with the background of this woman.

In those times, those things [lesbianism] were kind of simple and natural, and you didn't pay attention to it. I have this sketch I made of Aldous walking in the street—you know that the children in Florence are known to yell insults or remarks to people going by; they're very smart at that, and here's Aldous, long Aldous with his big Mexican hat—what he called the little Mexican—books under his arm, and probably shorts and sandals, walking on the sidewalk, and Maria and [her intimate friend] Constanza holding hands and walking behind him; and the little boys step in front of Aldous and say "Hey, are you taking them to school?"

Ellen Hovde (daughter-in-law)

The women who were lesbians in that time were women who were smart, independent, elegant, and worth talking to, and that all added up to a lot. It was also a time when they were trying to break down every barrier. I'm sure that Aldous and Maria and their circle tried every possible permutation and combination sexually that they could possibly think of because they felt it was their duty! They were trying it all, and that was quite new.

I remember Aldous speaking with relish about the bad old days when he was such a naughty young man, acerbic and witty and devilish and sort of putting pins in people in the Bloomsbury [London] period. He grinned from ear to ear, I mean he really did; he could be quite malicious, and he enjoyed it.

He liked being an icon-buster. He enjoyed that. It was one of the things I think he had in common with Julian who used to do things like dry salamanders in the sun, pinned down. Dreadful things. They were both capable of that.

Jeanne Neveux (sister-in-law Maria's elder sister)

At Lady Ottoline's nobody was dressed up in an official way as a fashion would [dictate]. Everybody tried something different and new.

To me, Garsington appeared very frightening because of all these people with the big names. I only stopped there for one or two nights, and I was very young. I can see the place. It was a lovely day, and we were out in the garden. Lady Ottoline was very impressive to me, but I was very pleased to go away as soon as possible.

Francis Huxley (nephew)

My mother [Juliette] tells me that Maria used to provide Aldous with psychological diagnoses of friends and acquaintances at parties, which Aldous would then string out into his novelistic form.

A lot of people told him, before he got married, that Maria was not who he should marry because she was otherwise inclined. I think to Maria it somehow all came together; I can't think that their sexual relationship was all that satisfying.

Maria, after all, was one of his greatest saviors in other senses: by the use of her intuition, by reading to him daily, by being his secretary-general, by looking after him in every particular.

Aldous first wished to be a doctor. You know how, in family lines, the line is seldom straight from father to son. It usually goes from grandfather to grandson. Or else, it does a knight's move to uncles. For some reason, Aldous had wished to be a doctor. He kept this interest all his life in some way—with his interest in alternative medicine.

When Aldous Huxley's first novel, *Crome Yellow,* was published in 1921, its setting was too explicit for the Morrell family, which is apparently caricatured in the work. Ottoline wrote him a scourging letter, one of many Huxley eventually received from family and friends protesting his too-direct references to aspects of their personal lives. His works shocked a whole generation of readers as well, quickly becoming the sort of literature read discreetly under the covers at night. The novels that followed—*Crome Yellow, Antic Hay, Those Barren Leaves*, as well as volumes of short stories and essays (Huxley was under contract to write three books a year)—established a literary reputation that would burgeon into worldwide fame with *Point Counter Point* (1928) and *Brave New World* (1932).

Naomi Mitchison (friend)

I remember my mama being rather shocked by his books, and *especially* by my reading them. I was sort of standing up to this and saying, "I'm not going to be stopped from reading Aldous's books." He was shocking the shockable people.

The worst things that he published were poems in Oxford's poetry annual. And pretty bad they are. Both of us were included in '15 and '16. We were very pleased to be in them. But they weren't very good poems.

Then he went to London. I went to London, too; but as a young married with a baby, I didn't see much of him. I helped him find some small place to live in London, just after they got married. There was a time when they were in London for a bit; they had a very great difficulty in finding a flat for a reasonable rent.

He asked me to find an inexpensive flat in London. I hunted about and sent him a note about one, and he snapped back, "You call that cheap?" Well, it wasn't. They were rather badly off, and I think that was in the early days of the marriage. I think he felt a bit deserted, and I don't think we had [deserted him]. I think they felt [poverty] quite differently, living in London, with the baby [Matthew], and so on. I was trying to get them all over. But I was living in relative riches compared with them; I think they considered it a break, which I was very sorry about.

Some people thought that he was . . . they wouldn't advise their females to read his books. But by the time, I was reading anything I could and bought all his books as they came out.

If you read the other things that were being written at that time, they don't seem to be about humans at all. He wrote about real people, and sometimes he'd laugh at them as well. They're really not funny. He was laughing about things that most people took terribly seriously.

One thing Aldous did was to put people into his books. Sometimes it was quite fun. My father comes into one or two of his books. Then there was one which I was in a bit. It hurt like mad. It was about a child that had died. He'd been watching me, I know, and he was tremendously sympathetic at the time. It was an awful business—our eldest son, and at that time nothing could be done. He [my son] died in a week, and nothing could be done. It went in the book [Point Counter Point].

I was rather upset about that because he was watching

me. But goodness, one does that; I mean, I've done it my-self. You watch people, and inevitably one puts in things which hurt, if one's writing a modern novel. It passed.

Francis Huxley (nephew)

His novels are full of malice, aren't they? You can get at what you dislike by caricaturing the situation and killing things publicly with little dark darts in which there are all kinds of undertones if you care to work them out. It's not bad to have written his father up in such a way that it caused disruptions in the family [in *Eyeless in Gaza*]: "Aldous, how could you have written about your father in such a way? We all know this was your father!"

"Oh, I didn't think that anyone would mind."

Starting in the mid-1920s, Aldous and Maria Huxley spent much of their time in southern Italy or southern France or traveling, such as the around-the-world tour that led to the publication of *Jesting Pilate* in 1926. "The feeling was that, partly, his eyesight didn't do as well in England; he couldn't live in England. He needed the sun," Juliette Huxley said in her interview. First in a suburb of Paris (Suresnes), then in Italy near Forte de Marmi, and finally in the South of France, in the little town of Sanary (near Toulouse), the Huxleys set up comfortable housekeeping in exile, returning to London annually to see family and friends and to attend to publish-ing business.

In these years Huxley built upon his growing reputation as a literary journalist, contributing hundreds of short pieces to *Vogue, Vanity Fair,* and the Hearst newspapers in the United States, all the while he turned out his dynamic early novels: *Antic Hay* (1923), *Those Barren Leaves* (1925), *Point Counter Point* (1928). Most of his short essays were collected in the period and published; but a few, particularly those espousing a eugenic agenda, have only recently come to light.[15] During this prolific period, one of the Huxleys' com-panions was Maria's sister, Jeanne.

Jeanne Neveux (sister-in-law)

I stayed with the Huxleys in the mid-1920s with my daughter, Sophie. They wanted to come and live in Paris, and I found a house for them on the outskirts of Paris in Suresnes, which is just on the other side of the Seine. It was, to me, a very easy life with maids and little things and meeting many, many people. But they soon, very soon, got sick of Paris and went to Italy, but first [stayed] in the South of France.

In Sanary they bought a house—the ugliest house on the coast, and they got it. They always got an ugly house; they never got a nice house. I don't know what they were like in America, but they were really gifted for just finding the wrong thing.

Naomi Mitchison (friend)

Aldous was not really political, but certainly moral. We were readers. We'd all read the sort of books which aren't read much now. We both cared quite a lot about science. And we would argue about history and morality. We were concerned about the way the world should be. We weren't too political, but we were preoccupied with morality.

[Later in the 1920s] my husband and I went down there to Sanary. That was great fun. We collected snails, Maria and I—I always liked her very much—between us we killed a scorpion. Aldous was very cross with us. He said, "You shouldn't have." We said, "Nonsense!" Aldous liked snails very much, so we teased him about cruelty at the expense of the snails.

It was a quite simple house, a rather nice garden with steps and a lot of interesting flowers. Lots of herbs and things, which she [Maria] used in cooking. She was a very good cook.

[Aldous had] just started painting. We often said, "Silly old Aldous." He was enjoying it, so . . . we were all sort of playing. When young grown-ups get together and get really fond of one another, it's very nice. It doesn't really matter what one does or what one says—and everything goes.

Aldous usually had a nod or two when he wasn't off painting or around writing. We went shopping. Occasionally we'd go out for a cup of coffee.

Juliette Huxley (sister-in-law)

When he left Balliol, he was looking for a job. And when he left Garsington (he stayed there six to eight months, as a worker on the land) and when Maria went away, he got a bit restless, and he tried to get this job [at the Air War Board in London].

He was not positively a conscientious objector, because both his best friend [Gielgud] and his cousin [Gervas] were in the war. And, he was British. There was this tremendous patriotism: "We must do all we can."

Julian came back from Houston, Texas, where he'd been professor of biology at Rice University between 1913 and 1916. In 1916, he wrote to Aldous. Aldous wrote back, "I shouldn't come back if I were you. Stay where you are. You can't do any good here." But Julian came back, nevertheless. He enlisted, spent about nine months training, and then was sent to Italy to join the Army as an Intelligence Officer. When[ever] he came to England, Julian came to Garsington—to stay, perhaps, or to come to a meal. He and Aldous were very, very much attached to each other. You see, Aldous was the younger brother, and, of course he was an invalid, with one eye, and very often ill, needing (and not claiming it, ever) a certain amount of care.

In World War I, Bertrand Russell was a pacifist of course and went to prison for that. Afterwards he sat on the pavement looking like a death's head—poor Bertie. Well, he had principles he felt he had to live up to. Pacifists then were people who could see that the whole thing was completely absurd and a destruction which could have been avoided. Every time I read a new book of Aldous's, I had a feeling of apprehension, because he peeled personalities to a painful surface sometimes. One had the feeling that he was almost corrosive. Most people cover up, don't they? And he took off. There was something vindictive in some of those early books.

We had a book by Jules Verne in our library which had belonged to the Huxley children at Prior's Field. That book had a picture of the dog falling down—Jules Verne's *Voyage to the Moon,* I think, in French, with illustrations. They showed the dog falling down in the void, spread out, and the little balloon going up. Aldous used exactly the same dog falling [on] the roof of the house in *Eyeless*.

Aldous [once] told me the story of his life. It was after ten o'clock, and my children had been put to bed; we'd had dinner, and we were sitting there on the roof looking at the full moon. It was a very convenient roof, with a staircase coming in, a door, then a flat lead surface, and then the eaves. We perched on the top. There was a moon, and these huge trees opposite.

Aldous started telling me how his mother and his brother had died. No self-pity. Never did Aldous utter one word of self-pity. Now your heart was [torn] to pieces, thinking of that child, exposed to all these calamities.

Matthew Huxley was born in 1920, while Aldous was struggling to make ends meet in London. Despite being an only child, he was shunted about during his earliest years, to Maria's family in Belgium and to boarding schools for progressive education, including Frensham Pond and Dartington. He spent his school holidays with family members in southern Europe and visited with them on their periodic returns to England.

In 1929, Aldous Huxley was introduced to Gerald Heard, a science writer whose specialty might best to be called the historical anthropology of consciousness.[16] He was seven years older than Aldous, from a family of Church of England adherents; Heard's Cambridge-trained intellect, strong in natural science and philosophy, was in many ways a complement to Huxley's background. The pair formed a cerebral friendship which lasted for decades, as Heard eventually accompanied the Huxley family to the U.S.

Jacob Zeitlin (bookseller and literary agent)

From the time that he met Gerald, he really was a disciple of Heard. Heard had two things: he was charming—I liked him very much—and he was brilliant. He was the most fluent and brilliant speaker I ever listened to. Words just came out; there was a continuous flow, so felicitous. His language and his reasoning were so good and so insidious.

Peggy Kiskadden (friend)

Gerald Heard used to lecture on the BBC on scientific subjects; he wrote for various magazines in England, and had written a book or two. He wrote several more when he came out here. He was extremely interested in religion but not in any particular sect. In fact, I think he had a real horror of sects as he was the son of a minister. So, his interest was always in matters pertaining to the life of the spirit.

He had very light blue eyes and they looked at you very hard. They were his most noticeable feature. He was very lean; he loved taking walks. He had a great sense of humor and was a delightful *raconteur*.

Christopher Isherwood (friend)

If you couldn't get hold of Bernard Shaw, perhaps Gerald Heard was the next best thing. He was a marvelous Irishman, with such an encyclopedia of information—such fascinating theories about everything. He was a great historical philosopher. In fact, he was in many respects the most fascinating person I've ever met.

Gerald was a beautiful man to look at. He had the most wonderful, pale-blue eyes that seemed almost sightless they were so far-looking into the future. In fact, he had fatal gifts in every way. He was really so overwhelmingly effective. One time at a party I saw some quite silly little boys who somehow or other got into conversation with him. He began telling them about the whole origins of mankind. I've never seen anything like the kind of hypnotized joy with which they were listening to all of this. I don't think they understood one word in six hundred, but that made no difference.

Oh, the beauty of his voice was outstanding. Melodious. I saw him on all kinds of occasions, public and private, and I never felt that he was less than on the level. He was very Irish and rather cultivated—had the brogue, you know. He was a marvelous speaker.

Juliette Huxley (sister-in-law)

Gerald Heard was one of those brilliant people. When we knew him, he was secretary to an Irishman (Sir Horace Plunkett) who traveled a great deal, also a very remarkable man. Then Gerald came to London. He was a homosexual, and he lived with a man called Christopher Wood—not the painter—another. They lived in Portman Square, and he was in with all kinds of ideas. A brilliant brain—perhaps a little bit inflammable? Aldous and Gerald traveled together a great deal, and when Aldous was dying, Gerald came. They had a pact. When one of them was about to die or be very sick, the other one would come and tell him. Now Gerald wasn't going to tell Aldous that he was going to die. He never did. You could say that their relationship was fraternal.

But you can't compare it to his relationship with Julian, can you? You see, Julian was a brother. He had been a great influence in Aldous's childhood. There was much more link between them—their mother, for instance, and their father. A family link is something quite different than an intellectual link. Gerald Heard and Aldous were very good friends and understood each other fully, but they hadn't got the family. (I don't know about family, because my family didn't link up with me like that.) But those two Huxleys were linked. They both were polymaths, and there was nothing that Julian would bring out that Aldous didn't know something about—nor anything that Aldous brought out that Julian did not know something about. And the field was very wide.

Peggy Kiskadden (friend)

Matthew, who is now thoroughly Americanized despite his strong accent, never had the kind of father relationship that most American boys have. It was more the English type. But at least an English boy grows up to go shooting with his father or to cricket matches with him. Matthew never had any of that. They would go on walks and Aldous would talk with Matthew. It was never a matter of sloughing Matthew off; it was that neither of them were equipped to be parents.

The burden of being Aldous's son—even when he was little—gave him [Matthew] this tremendous burden which Aldous was not aware of at all. Aldous was the soul of sweetness, but it's an awful thing to be Aldous's son. In those days it was *Brave New World* and *Point Counter Point,* which were on everybody's tongue, and Matthew (as a little boy) didn't know what the dickens that was all about.

Maria got very upset when he wrote *Point Counter Point.* There's a child in there, and at the end the child dies. Maria was very upset because the child was the same age as their son. It's the only time that she reproached him: to have done something like that which had no interest in the book—why did this child have to die?[17]

Chapter II
Hollywood (1937–1941)

In the mid-1930s, Huxley suffered from writer's block and physical collapse while finishing his experimental (and most autobiographical) novel *Eyeless in Gaza*. A niece recalls him as "stooped, intense, sort of tortured." The international success of *Brave New World* in 1932 became a burden to live up to, rather than a pleasurable triumph.

As a young man Aldous Huxley cared supremely "for knowledge for its own sake, for the play of ideas, for the arts of literature, painting and music." By the midpoint of his life, his pleasure in aesthetics waned. "For some years now I have felt a certain dissatisfaction with these things . . . these activities of the mind can be seen in their true perspective when looked at from the vantage point of mysticism. 'Those barren leaves of science and of art' are barren only when regarded as ultimate ends."[1]

To his son Matthew, the mid-1930s represented a time when his father converted to a spiritually oriented pacifism; when for the first time Aldous Huxley realized the implications of political and nationalist repression firsthand. What then should he believe in?

World War I had horrified Huxley with its carnage; many, perhaps half of his classmates at Eton and at Oxford had died.[2] Yet at this time his abhorrence of war found outlet in satires of the mores of his era, rather than in overt political statements.

By 1935, Huxley had, in effect, run out of cynicism; he became a prominent pacifist lecturer associated with Reverend Dick Sheppard's Oxford Peace Pledge campaign. Meditation, physical rehabilitation therapies, and a cause worth believing in (pacifism) finally lifted his writer's block. His agonies would not end so easily. No sooner was his illness and writer's block cured (and *Eyeless in Gaza* published) than his former pacifist friends attacked him for refusing to endorse military force to defend the Spanish Republic.[3]

After the jibes grew shrill, Huxley departed with his family and Gerald Heard to lecture on pacifism. They drove south from New York across the U.S.A. to New Mexico, where on D. H. Lawrence's ranch, Huxley wrote his still-classic argument against war, *Ends and Means*. Then Aldous and Maria visited Hollywood, ostensibly only for a little while, to sell Huxley's works to the film studios.

Juliette Huxley (sister-in-law)

I knew Aldous was going through troubles in 1935. He couldn't write anymore. He had insomnia as well—a very difficult period. He was having trouble with his teeth, also his eyes. He couldn't sleep and he couldn't eat very well. Not being able to work was almost like not being able to breathe for him, because all these Huxleys were addicted to work—from the grandfather. I think Aldous tried various things, and finally it was [the physical rehabilitation techniques of] F. M. Alexander who pulled him together.

You see, Aldous's silences were always dominant. He would sit there with a lot of people, talking—all the people talking—and then Aldous would be silent. Gradually the silence would spread, like a wave. It was very curious. Everybody could be affected by a silence like that. I think he felt disabled, in a way, to compete with all this chatter. He didn't want to. And he retired in himself.

Francis Huxley (nephew)

He went to see F. Mathias Alexander for a time because, I've been told, when he was born his head was so large that he found it very difficult to stand upright, and he used to fall over backwards with his vast cerebral weight. Being six foot four, and an ectomorph at that, he was rather spindly. So he went to see Alexander. I think this was a very well-intentioned endeavor on both their parts, but I used to have the feeling, watching Aldous walk, that he was aiming at being so upright, he actually leaned backwards slightly as he walked.

Peggy Kiskadden (friend)

By the mid-1930s, he had gotten into Rev. Dick Sheppard, who was working so hard to deflect the British government and the British people from saying a war is [was] coming; they were just feeling it's [was] inevitable. He and Gerald Heard and others worked very hard in this Peace Pledge Union, made speeches, and then saw that it was hopeless and that you couldn't budge [Europe]. They felt maybe something could be done in America. They came over originally on a speaking tour. They were on the same program. Gerald had a very fluent tongue and no difficulty at all in talking, and Aldous would stand there moon-faced, and hardly be able to get anything out. He became fluent at the end of his life. (If you've ever heard the talks he gave at the University at Santa Barbara, they're extremely good lectures.) But when he first came over, in 1937, he found it very hard [to lecture]. He always had [his talk] written.

Aldous had been working trying to convince people that there had to be a better way than killing to resolve the problems between nations. They saw war coming, and they had been working very hard against it.

Naomi Mitchison (friend)

The move away from pacifism [in 1936] was a curious business, and some very good people were involved. It was always very difficult to make up one's mind. [There were] a few people who managed to combine both being on the right side in Spain and being pacifist. Very few people seemed to get it right. I think Aldous was fairly careful with what was going to be remembered in his writing. But between times, of course, one went to meetings and one went on writing things and signing things.

The thing about Aldous was that he couldn't have served anyhow [in World War II]. By that time he was getting into middle age; he was past forty.

A lot of the Black Shirts [under the leadership of Oswald Mosley] were having this great do [at London's Olympia Theatre], and we decided we were going to break it up. Some of us were Left in the politics of one kind or another; I was at that time quite deep in the Labour Party; also I was very shocked at the Fascists—what they were going to do, especially in London, where so many of them lived. The row was run mostly by Labour Party people. Our enemies were partly the Black Coats—the Fascists. Also we had [some trouble] with the police, because the police tended to go for anybody who was fighting anybody else, and one had to sit rather still.

We were somewhere near one another; we were mostly up on the first balcony.

I wasn't worried that Aldous would be hurt or attacked, really. There were quite a lot of people who would be looking after him. The police were arresting people without looking very much at what they were doing. We all kept an eye on one another. We all were yelling and occasionally throwing things. Aldous, too. Everybody was. It was partly the excitement. And, of course, we were young and frightened. We were dodging not only our enemies, but also the police. We didn't want to get arrested.

Christopher Isherwood (friend)

People in England may have thought Aldous's move to the U.S. was just "a failure of nerve," a very popular expression at that time—meaning that you'd lost belief in God knows what, life or something.

I don't think anybody ever questioned Huxley's integrity. As for his pacifism, he had declared that earlier [in 1935, Aldous joined Rev. Sheppard's Peace Pledge Union; on December 3, he made his first address on pacifism]. I just happened to run into a nest of pacifists when I got out here. There was a remarkable man named Alan Hunter, a Congregationalist minister at a church in Hollywood.

Remember, Aldous and Gerald's pacifism had been publicly stated years before in their writings. They were absolutely above suspicion of any kind as far as that was concerned. They wouldn't have been drafted if they'd been the last troops available. Good God help the United States if they had been! That was the feeling.

After the trip to China [1934–1935], [W. H.] Auden and I really wanted to be together more and more. We wanted to have more adventures. So our dream was to return immediately to America—that had very much taken our fancy. We imagined we were going to settle in New York for ever and ever, I think. That's what we thought. We were very happy-go-lucky in those days, as one is when one's still relatively young.

I knew perfectly well we'd be at home in Hollywood because of the variety of people. I spent a certain amount of time in Germany [1929–1933]. My chief friends while there were German Jews, whom I then met again after Hitler came into power. They'd emigrated hastily, many of them to England. So I got to know a lot of people, and in this way I was *persona grata* with a whole bunch of people who regarded me as though I'd practically been part of the resistance to the Nazis. I was absolutely in solid. People said, "Oh we all know Chris; he's an honorary Jew," one of the greatest compliments I ever had paid to me. By the most charming, delightful coincidence, these Jews turned out to be in very important positions in film studios. I became great friends with people, particularly Godfrey Reinhardt, the son of [director] Max Reinhardt. There was never any question. It didn't hurt that I was a writer, but I actually got jobs with great facility.

I didn't really realize that I would take this man as seriously as I did later. But then, I hadn't met Huxley. I thought, and an enormous majority of people, I'm sorry to say, thought at that time that he was a mountainously remote, icy intellectual.

Aldous was a person who was very much into being exact—saying what you mean, saying what are the exact facts. Aldous was very, very British and Gerald was very, very Irish. It's perfectly true that Gerald floated off into great flights of talk. He was one of the most marvelous talkers. [He brought] the hint of an entirely different way of life, of an entirely different way of thinking.

Aldous was very, very gentle. Images of tallness come in—the giraffe, except that he didn't look at all silly. He had a very strange effect in his eyes, which were defective; although in actual practical life, he got around perfectly well.

Like most British people, he fell madly in love with the California outdoors. Many of us were deeply concerned because, as you well know, you can't go striding into tall grass in this country without at least hearing a great deal of rattling [from a rattlesnake] going on. Nevertheless, he became one of the great enthusiasts of California's scenery. He and his wife knew all these places, and walked miles—traveled by car and rode horseback. They were a wonderful pair.

Peggy Kiskadden (friend)

In the mid-1930s, the Huxleys' son Matthew was at Dartington [Hall] at school, and so they would come down frequently to see him, and I met them at the Elmhursts', the founders of Dartington. I knew Gerald Heard better than Aldous; the three of them came to this country and let me know right away. I happened to be in New York and I saw them there, as they arrived off the boat. Then I went on west. When they came west, they came to us the first night [for] dinner. We saw a great deal of each other after that.

[On arrival] they were full of different things they'd seen—everything from Florida crackers to western types. They felt America was so vital and alive—as many English people do when they first come. [Why were they coming to Hollywood?] I think it was both tourism and that the climate seemed so good. Aldous had always had a tendency to bronchial troubles and Maria, who was very fearful of this, felt that this would be a wonderful climate for him. Then they moved out to the desert, feeling that dry air would be better for Aldous. He had contracted pneumonia twice.

The Huxleys were interested in the States and very amused by Hollywood. They drove all around America before they came out here, but it tickled them very much: some of the movie stars and the goings-on they felt were as good as a play. They felt quite detached from it—and enjoyed it.

I found them rooms at a hotel that was called The Garden of Allah. Now it's torn down, but it was a nice small hotel with a garden around it. There were some cottages behind, and we reserved a cottage for them there. That was quite close to where I lived, so we settled them in there, and then they came up to our house for dinner.

That first supper, I remember having a desperate feeling that I didn't remember whether they were vegetarians, and so, when the roast was passed, I turned to my left and to my right and said, "If you don't eat meat, please leave it." And they did. When it was passed to me, I left it. Four or five months later, when we all knew each other very much better, and were on a picnic together, it transpired that we'd all become vegetarians that night. Naturally we'd all been thinking about it, and it just took someone to say, "Don't eat it if you don't want it" to tip them over.

Aldous and Gerald went on a speaking tour the next winter, after they arrived in the summer. They spoke all around various places in this country. I think that by that time

America was pretty well alerted, at least thoughtful people were, that there was grave danger of war.

Jacob Zeitlin (bookseller and literary agent)

I had met Frieda Lawrence in early 1937, and she had been told that I was the man who could sell the Lawrence manuscripts. So, she and Angelino came to see me. She said that she had the manuscripts in a trunk out in New Mexico at the Ranch, and she would like me to consider taking them on to sell: come there, see the manuscripts, and discuss terms for selling and so on. So I went [that summer], and Aldous and Maria were there, living in one of the cottages. When I met them, they were the palest, most fragile-looking people I ever saw. They looked like they hadn't been out in the sun in years. Their skin was transparent. It was quite a contrast to what became of them both after they had moved to California.

We met at breakfast, and I remember that Frieda and Angelino had cooked up a pumpkin-blossom omelet, which was one of their favorite dishes, and it really was very good, very tender pumpkin blossoms. The talk was just of this and that. Later, I sat down, and as I say, I asked Huxley what he was working on. He talked quite at length. You know, Aldous Huxley, when he got started, was not a brief talker.

Angelino told me that one night he woke up and he could hear a typewriter going "tap tap tap tap" and couldn't see any lights in any of the cottages. Finally he traced it to the cottage they were in, and Aldous was sitting here in the dark, typing. Because he was a touch-typist anyway. He couldn't see well enough to see the keys, so he didn't need to. And he was sitting there in the dark, typing. At that time, he was working on *Ends and Means*. I said, "What are you working on? I know that it's a question everybody asks you, but I'm just curious whether you're working on another work of fiction," and he told me about *Ends and Means*.

"Now," I said to Aldous, "I don't know what your plans

are, but if you want to come to Hollywood, I have a connection with one of the most important agencies there, and I can introduce you to the head of their department that sells literary materials, and I'm sure they could get you the best possible fees and they're responsible, respectable agents." That was the William Morris Agency. Later I wrote to him, and I said, "Without making any commitments on your part, if you are interested, I'll be glad to put you in touch with these people." So then he wrote me back, and he did come out. I introduced him to Jim Geller and Billy Morris. Jim Geller was head of the literary department of the William Morris Agency (which was mainly a theatrical agency, but did handle some writers).

We went down to Santa Fe and picked up [the poet] Witter Bynner and went to the Santo Domingo Rain Dance: Aldous and Maria, [Matthew], Frieda Angelino, and Witter Bynner. The curious thing is that it did rain like hell—when the rain dance was over, the rain came down, a gully-washer. I remember Aldous saying that someday people will be saying that this rain dance is to celebrate the end of World War I. People's notions change, and they forget the historical origins of things.

Maria was a person that you couldn't fail but notice; she seemed to have everything well in hand. She was a decisive person, but not aggressive. She'd make you aware of her concern for Aldous all the time. She never let up in her watching out for him. She would wash the clothes while Aldous typed most of his manuscripts and then corrected them by hand. She often would do the final draft, the final typewritten script.

I think Aldous took Maria for granted—she did everything. She drove the car, she did the shopping, and she looked after him; he was her child. So much so, in fact, that she told Josephine, my wife, that the thing to do was to get children out of the way. Aldous's career was everything, and that's the way they made Matthew feel. When they got over here, they put Matthew in a boarding school up in Colorado, and Matthew, I think, suffered greatly from that. But, she just told him, very bluntly, "Aldous comes first." I think she realized she had a genius on her hands, and she was going to help him achieve his fullest possibilities.

When he first came out here he was staying at the Roosevelt Hotel. Initially, just for a few days. Maria wasn't with him when he came out the first time.

Huxley told William Morris, Jr., "Well, I'm sorry but my agent sold that [*Brave New World*] to RKO last year, for 750 pounds." Aldous didn't even get that money; it had been sold. We tore our hair, and went on to something else.

Dorris Halsey (agent)

Huxley came to Hollywood as a prestige writer. There was a wartime influx of the intelligentsia of Europe, the Thomas Manns and Aldous Huxleys and Leon Feuchtwangers. There was a whole coterie of the Europeans, including Christopher Isherwood, of course.

During those days you had literate producers; you were not gearing the scripts to the lowest common denominator. You were not catering to the twelve-year-olds. That was still the golden age, slightly tarnished nevertheless, of Hollywood.

Huxley was inordinately tall, as you can tell from the photographs, and stooped down to most people. People were in awe as they would be of their school principal. They didn't dare open their mouths for fear that ungrammatical words might creep out. I myself was in awe, but I had the excuse of English not being my language. He spoke French to me on a number of occasions.

Ellen Hovde (daughter-in-law)

Matthew used to complain bitterly that people would always say, "Oh, you're a Huxley, well, what do you do? Who are you?" He always felt that he had to be something that he wasn't. That's what I mean by being the son of not only a famous man, but from a famous family. It's a killer.

Aldous had broken from all that, and it didn't exist in our part of the family. Aldous didn't even believe in teaching people Latin, eventually. I think that he was much more a person of the new world than the old, although he wouldn't have said so. He also was, of course, incredibly European, but in terms of what he thought about the way he felt about taking risks, it was a real break with those traditions.

Jacob Zeitlin (bookseller and literary agent)

Aldous was involved with a curious crowd of people in England. Some of them were, of course, intellectuals and pacifists and the crowd at Ottoline Morrell's place.

After he was here awhile, I think he realized that he could never, number one, earn as much money [elsewhere], which he well deserved to earn because he had really starved in England. He was making a living writing criticism and short essays, and these books hadn't yet sold to the extent that they brought him enough royalties to live off of decently. They were really miserably poor a good part of the time over there.

I think the second consideration was his health. He was never as healthy as he was in southern California. I don't think I ever heard him talk of leaving here. He bought a house here; he bought property here and out on the desert. I don't think he had any intention of returning.

Aldous Huxley was a magic name. It always was. It's a curious thing: from the time he was a young man and wrote his first book, he was an internationally famous man who was supposed to represent the younger generation of people who really knew what it was all about. By the time Aldous got here he had a great reputation as a travel writer and essayist. A lot of people had never read anything he wrote but cultivated him anyway because his name implied being right among the smart people.

Around the publication of *Ends and Means* Aldous lost his following. It was evident to me from the remarks of people that came into the bookshop. First of all, they felt that he was flirting with fads, and the next thing was that he'd given up all of his *Antic Hay* [satire] and that he was getting serious. Now they didn't understand that he was serious all the time that he was being satirical, and he really was not being funny when he described these people. When he actually announced his seriousness, started to write things like *Eyeless in Gaza,* they said well, this isn't what I expect of Aldous Huxley. I think that *Point Counter Point* was the last [of the satires] and actually the turning point. A lot of people thought it was far too serious.

Huxley referred to Neville Chamberlain as a "wretch." He also referred to the people in Europe who were faced by all that Hitler's movement had turned loose as "wretches." But, somehow or another, it's a curious thing, he almost had a Christian Science attitude toward the people who were in misery or suffering: it was because they had entertained evil thought. It's hard to say that about a whole continent. Well, he told the story about the priest who used to go aboard the slave ships and try to help the misery of the slaves that were being transported to America. They would stop in Spain on the way from Africa, and these priests would go on. They would not only minister to them, that is, give them water and food, try and treat their sicknesses, but they would also preach to them of the depravity of their souls which had brought them to this condition.

I heard Aldous and Gerald speak, yes, down at the L.A. Philharmonic Auditorium [October 18, 1937]; it was the first one they gave when they started their tour. Gerald, of course, was very fluent and spoke without notes. Aldous had to read his—it would be typed with a large typewriter on a piece of paper and then he would hold it up like this (against his eyes) to read from. So Aldous was not a very moving public speaker.

There are some people who have the idea that Huxley should have stayed in England and led the pacifist movement. I think he very wisely decided that it was like trying to stop the sea. The other thing was that in Britain he was not in very good health, and the conditions under which they would have to live would not be very good. He didn't like to become involved in a war because he didn't believe in war; on the other hand, he didn't want to be labeled a traitor to England. So he concluded that he could do more good for the cause that he was now interested in. He believed that the roots of war came out of the lack of a proper sense of man's relationship to the universe and the divine essence; and, if anything could be accomplished, it could be accomplished through teaching and trying to develop a kind of fundamental spirit in which war would not be an alternative.

As I remember [when he returned to California the second time, after the speaking tour], he got pneumonia and was very sick. In fact, that was before antibiotics, and they had him under an oxygen tent. He was in very bad shape. He got chilled, and his lungs weren't very strong, so he was desperately ill for a while.

Jeanne Neveux (sister-in-law)

Aldous foresaw the war. He really saw the war arriving and he tried in London, I don't know what his actions were, but I know that he did everything to foretell it, try to explain what to do, and so on. When he realized he could do nothing—he must have done some talks in London at the time— and when he saw that he was of no use, he was asked to go to America, and he accepted. Although they were not so anxious [to go]; they didn't like America that much. It was not the place they would have lived. They would have lived in England; they would've lived in Italy; but they didn't like America so much. They went there because they knew the war was arriving. They wanted me intensely to go there, because of the war, you see. Well, they did not intend to stay—they dreaded that maybe they would have to.

Jacob Zeitlin (bookseller and literary agent)

His first film job was with MGM [August 1938]. I remember going out to see him there once, and he said, "They also serve who only sit and wait," paraphrasing Milton.

The studio people were all curious about him. They put him in their writers' building; they gave him a dog kennel like all the rest, and they put one of the best people in the studios to work with him, to give him an idea of how they did it. I think it was Madaline Ruthven. [Huxley also worked with Jane Murfin at MGM.[4]] She was a poetess. She was the one that they always assigned to indoctrinate the best writers that came in. When Faulkner came out here, they put him with her.

One of the quandaries in evaluating the success of Huxley's Hollywood years is the extent to which he meshed with the professional film community there. Was he a "fish out of water," as the Huxleys' new friend Peggy Kiskadden thought, or did he do his screenwriting with professional grace and aplomb, as Christopher Isherwood believed? There can be no doubt that Huxley helped write screenplays that critics call some of the most literary in Hollywood history: *Madame Curie* (which F. Scott Fitzgerald also scripted), *Pride and Prejudice, Jane Eyre,* and *Alice in Wonderland.* Huxley was not merely a prestige name on these projects; his drafts, some available to scholars, show consistent progress toward professional screenwriting standards.

Yet without the help of Jacob Zeitlin and Anita Loos (arguably the first professional screenwriter in the industry) Huxley would not have gotten far. Zeitlin introduced him to the William Morris Agency, which subsequently represented his film work. Loos was then under contract at Metro-Goldwyn-Mayer, and her datebook for this period shows that she arranged frequent meetings between Aldous and MGM executives. Within six months after the Huxleys' arrival in Los Angeles, Aldous was attending the brunches and dinner parties of Anita Loos, who lived within shouting distance of both W. R. Hearst and Irving Thalberg, perhaps MGM's most respected producer. He also appeared at the salon for literary *émigrés* informally hosted by Salka Viertel, whose guests included the brothers Mann, Bertolt Brecht, and Greta Garbo. (Huxley's simultaneous frailty and notoriety is documented in his caricature as "Boxley" in Fitzgerald's *The Last Tycoon.*)

The film stars of the Huxley circle were Charlie Chaplin and Paulette Goddard, Chaplin's putative wife; Orson Welles, who once borrowed a convertible in use on a gangster film to impress Aldous and Maria (who were inordinately fond of cars); Greta Garbo, for whom Huxley wrote his version of *Madame Curie;* actress Constance Collier; actor Burgess Meredith; screenwriter Charles McArthur, and, of course, Anita Loos. Gerald Heard, Christopher Isherwood, Edwin Hubble (the distinguished astronomer) and his wife, Grace, and, later, Igor Stravinsky composed the rest of their circle.[5]

Ellen Hovde (daughter-in-law)

Maria was the most elegant creature, without ever following fashion. She was always incredibly elegant, very tiny, very small-boned and dark. She wore a lot of close-fitting clothes.

Isherwood, a friend of David Hockney, was very reserved and very, very English. He and Aldous used to discuss where they bought their jackets. Other people would talk seriously, but there would be an undercurrent like, "Umm, like your jacket, where'd you get it?" He did seem very fond of Aldous, but they had that "very proper" attitude with each other.

They were not bosom buddies, but that was not their style. I think that Aldous was certainly closer to Gerald Heard than he was to Christopher. Christopher was more wary, perhaps. He suffered from feeling that he hadn't done as well as he might, in terms of being a man of letters.

Anita was chatty. She would make conversation, and she knew everyone. She was extremely funny, and also biting, which Aldous was, too. He loved that kind of thing; it was great, great fun. He liked gossip. Of course Maria was the grand champion at social news, and all these people were her close friends.

Peggy Kiskadden (friend)

Anita did a great deal, I think, for Aldous when he first came out. I'm sure that her fine Italian hand had to do with his working in some of the pictures, being employed as a writer.

The studios were a new experience. He was interested in the work, and everybody was awfully nice to him. It was a perfectly pleasant experience, but he was awfully glad to get back to his own writing. He was a solitary writer. He would write all morning, sitting out in the ramada.

They were great friends with Anita Loos, and the reason they were friends was that when she wrote the book *Gentlemen Prefer Blondes*, Aldous had read it, and he wrote her a fan letter [in 1927].[6] She was so flattered that this writer in England had paid attention to her that she wrote back. She was a very witty, intelligent woman.

Anita Loos was the pivot of the Huxleys' social circle; she introduced them to Charlie Chaplin and to all the various people that were interesting in the movie world at that time. They found that quite fascinating. At the same time, Aldous was very interested in various professors from California Institute of Technology and from UCLA.

The Hubbles were wonderful. Edwin Hubble was a great astronomer, and Grace Hubble was a dear. We went to Mount Wilson several times with them and looked through the great telescope.

Edwin Hubble was tall and good-looking and very well educated, very able to talk with Gerald and Aldous and [was] fascinated by them. They were utterly fascinated by him. They wanted to find out everything they could about astronomy. There would be very interesting talks. I think Aldous's interest in astronomy was much more profound than Gerald's. Gerald was interested—and with his good

English education was perfectly competent to understand what he heard, but Aldous was a scholar. I always felt that was the difference.

Gerald was wonderful in asking questions; I suppose he'd had a lot of experience on the BBC. Aldous would sit there with that sort of moon-like expression which was accentuated because of the eyes which didn't look quite normal, and Gerald would just ply him with questions.

I remember one time at Salka Viertel's, when Aldous was there and Greta Garbo and several people. Chaplin was trying out all these little routines on us to see which ones we laughed at. I've never had more fun in my life. He did just the gestures, and he was just a great actor in his particular genre. We sat there while Greta Garbo sat on the couch. My husband [William Kiskadden] was there, very tall; you just knew when you looked at him he was a doctor. And I heard this voice saying, "Tell me, doctor," and I moved right off so Garbo could have the center of the stage. She enjoyed it.

It was Easter [1939]. We all went on a picnic. We all drove out somewhere and it was in a grove of trees—probably up in the Hollywood Hills somewhere. It was a lovely day and a lovely picnic.

Krishnamurti came and also Rosalind Rajagopal and her husband. Chris Isherwood came. I think Maria had purchased a young goat (it was Easter), feeling that it was the time to celebrate birth and new beings.

There were perhaps twelve of us and you wouldn't want to descend on nature en masse, so we went in different directions. We met somewhere and followed each other to a place that one of us knew—a meadow somewhere in one of the canyons far up. Everybody brought something, and we ate. Then we went on walks in different directions.

Betty Wendel (friend)

What attracted him about working with the studios was the money. [Yet] he thought he was terribly overpaid and felt terribly guilty about it. Anita said, "Well, just remember, you can send the money to the family over there." And he did. He liked the movie people; he just didn't like writing for the movies.

Siggy Wessberg (nephew-in-law)

I think he laughed at California, but I think he enjoyed it. He always enjoyed the freedom of it. He was taken in by some of the crazy fads and some of the things they had there. I think he liked the easy California style. It suited him.

Jacob Zeitlin (bookseller and literary agent)

Actually, Aldous, right from the first, thought that the story about the nuns [*Devils of Loudun*] might be the most suitable for films [long before he wrote his book]. I don't think he thought of himself as being employed to adapt or to write screenplays. He gave us what he thought was a scenario [*Success*], and it was so bad, we never showed it to anybody. I think the only surviving copy is the one I have. *Success* was about the Chicago stockyards, and it was just no good at all. We thought it better not to sell it, to leave a better impression.

As I understand it, they [MGM] came to him and they said, "Look, we've got your job and the price is $2,500 a week," and he said, "Good God, I can't take that much, I'm not worth it." It was Anita Loos who said to him, "Look, you've got family and friends in Europe and England, and they're starving. Just think of how much money you could send them, what it would mean to them in the way of money and other help." That was a good argument; it persuaded him.

Anita was a very little woman, and she wore her hair as you see it in the pictures, with the bangs across the front. She was very straightforward and bright. She was intuitively adaptable and quick to sense other people and what they were like. She was certainly alert, more than ordinarily alert.

[Huxley's attitude toward work in Hollywood?] He hoped they would assign him to something that he could do, was qualified to do. They wanted him to work on Somerset Maugham's *Of Human Bondage* and he said, "I may be an English author, but I'm not that kind of author." He really despised Maugham, and he had something of a similar attitude toward Galsworthy. They wanted him, for instance, to work on *The Forsythe Saga* and he said, "No." So, finally the big job that they put him on was a script about Madame Curie.

Well, he rather liked that idea; he thought it was a challenge. Because, you see, Madame Curie had her public life, and then she had her private life. According to the stories that circulated, she had a number of lovers; and you could make something out of that if you were very careful. She had the outward image of a saint, [but] her laboratory assistant was picked up to sleep with. The fact is, she was just as human as anybody else.

There was no doubt that several studios wanted Huxley. They wanted him because he was Aldous Huxley; they never felt they got their money's worth out of what he produced for them. It was prestige they were after.

Christopher Isherwood (author)

I think studios were terribly proud of Aldous; they thought he gave them class. Whatever else Aldous was or wasn't, he was certainly an aristocrat. He was really very stylish and so nice. He knew about everything. He was supporting his loved ones, just like the rest of us. He had to earn this money. He got serious, interested in this because it was something to be done. So he'd made up his mind he was going to be interested. And, of course, he made it sound absolutely fascinating when he talked about these pictures.

They greatly respected him and were proud to have him. On top of that, it was no shit: he really could do it. "He subdued the dyer's hand to what it works in." He was very good in that way. The studios were trying to get us to write one together. I can't remember. I don't even think there's the slightest record of it [*Jacob's Hands*, 1944, unpublished]. But the usual epitaph—which is more satisfactory than the usual epitaphs usually are—is that we got paid.

Peggy Kiskadden (friend)

Gerald and his partner, [the pianist] Christopher Wood, knew that their homosexuality wasn't of any importance to me [and it was common in the film community]. They could have had seven wives and it wouldn't have been of any importance. I liked *them*. Whatever their personal life was didn't matter in the least to me. I felt like Mrs. Patrick Campbell, who said she didn't care what people did "so long as they didn't frighten the horses." I applaud that attitude.

The Hollywood people thought, "Aldous Huxley: Oh goodness, wonderful," and then he would be employed and would work on a script. Nobody understood what he was saying because they like something that even a kindergartner would understand. Aldous at that point was very, very English and very donnish and what he had to say, in the way of dialogue, couldn't be understood by an American, especially the particular American audience that the movies slant toward. They [Hollywood folk] were terribly in awe of him, but they found him so erudite that he was just miles away from them. So he never was a real success in writing. He made some money, which was very useful at that time, but he really was never a great success at writing for the movies. I just knew that the dialogue Aldous would write would simply not do. He really was a fish out of water at MGM. He was an ornament to them; they liked saying that he was working there, but they really couldn't use his work very well.

Lawrence Powell (librarian)

[How did Huxley fit into Hollywood?] Well, he saw it as a source of income. I think he was interested in the people always, and the women. When he worked on Jane Austen and other things, I think he was very interested in the human side of it. He was a novelist, let's face it. He wasn't an historian, *he wasn't a scholar*. He primarily thought of himself as a novelist, an essayist. I don't think he regarded himself as demeaning himself by working there. He took life straight across.[7]

Perhaps the last word on Huxley's success in Hollywood belongs to his son Matthew, who recalls that his father was fascinated with the notion of making a lot of money easily, as in his Hollywood script "Success." "For him, Hollywood was always hard work to do. In his heart of hearts, it was a mysterious, totally improbable way of making money: he always hoped to hit it big."[8]

In the autumn of 1939, the Huxleys had settled in Santa Monica Canyon, then the center of literary exile life in Los Angeles. In that green, lush gorge that separates Santa Monica from Pacific Palisades, among the sycamore, oak, and palm trees, lived Isherwood, Heard, Garbo, and Thomas Mann— down the road from the Huxleys' home on Amalfi Drive. There Huxley threw a publication party to celebrate his first American novel (a parody of tycoons in general and Hearst in particular), *After Many a Summer Dies the Swan,* at the end of 1939. The recently arrived Orson Welles attended; six months later *he* was circulating a script on Hearst, *Citizen Kane*. Their life in the expatriate community is recollected by the niece of Anita Loos, Mary Anita.

Mary Anita Loos (friend)

Anita lived on the oceanfront called the Gold Coast. She had a beautiful house built by Richard Neutra, near all of the motion picture people who worked at the studios. My father lived in the Canyon, which was about a mile from where Anita's house was. When the war began, and shortly before, all of the refugees flocked into this area. Many of them had spent their holidays in Italy and Spain when they lived in London and in the central part of Europe because it was cheap. [Santa Monica Canyon] reminded them of Italy: the climate, the general living, the food and so on.

Aldous found a little cottage up on Amalfi Drive, and it was absolutely the thing that he had in Europe—a fig tree to sit under, a bench and a redwood table where we would sit and eat cheese, bread, pick figs off the tree, and eat oranges, and talk.

[My aunt] Anita adored him; they had an intellectual relationship. Anita was adamant about being an intellectual. She got to know the Huxleys at this time, and when Aldous came here, as many did during the war, she was all set to appreciate somebody she could really talk to. Huxley at this particular time was close to Dr. Hubble and his wife, Grace. Dr. Hubble was working at Palomar on this immense lens (just before he had gone to work in an army weapons laboratory).

I would call the Amalfi Drive house a beach bungalow. It had a garden in front, and at that time the street was very much a country street. It seems to me that when we sat out there, and had our wine and our cheese and bread and fruit, that it was absolutely country living. Furnishings didn't mean much. If they had anything on the walls it was just simply because somebody had given it to them— something of Man Ray [surrealist photographer] made out of wood, or it might be a painting of somebody that was really very good. I don't think they ever bothered to have it framed in any special way. Possessions weren't theirs. They lived in the world of the mind.

Occasionally Aldous would get a job at a studio, which was always kind of a disaster. Anita pushed very hard to get jobs for him because he was so brilliant. They really had no money. I don't know why Huxley's books didn't do very well; of course, the very famous one did well. *After Many a Summer Dies the Swan* was a success because it was about Hearst.

Aldous had a big crush on Paulette Goddard. He thought that she was the epitome of glamour. And he was amused at her capers. George Gershwin was in love with her. And she had this big thing with [Anatole] Litvak, and Charlie was suffering all over the place.

While she was with Charlie, we all used to go to Charlie's house. It was kind of grim, but Paulette was full of fun. It was a house done in a great deal of upholstered, heavy furniture, and a three-way organ with the pipes, old-fashioned, 1920s and 1930s splendor. She was such a madcap, so crazy, and Aldous thought she was divine. So his whole concept of the sexy woman in *After Many a Summer* is based on Paulette. She was most comely in appearance, with that beautiful hair and eyes and fair skin. She was a sex object of her time. She absolutely drove people crazy, and she had a very, very amusing and funny way. She was a collector. She liked jewels, she liked gems—and, she was a gold digger. For instance, she'd play golf with Howard Hughes and say, "I bet you five thousand dollars that you can't . . ." do this or that while they were playing golf. If he didn't do it, she said, "You owe me five thousand." If she didn't do it, she said, "Ha ha!"

Burgess Meredith (actor)

Paulette was just very fast, very witty, uninhibited, and very aware of what went on in people's minds, and kept it bubbling. She loved and knew how to handle witty men [like Aldous] and wise people; one knows her by the people she went with: aside from Chaplin and Wells—that was all before—then later with Eric [Maria] Remarque. She and Aldous were fast friends.

Christopher Isherwood (friend)

Charlie Chaplin was just about to shoot *The Great Dictator*, and he acted out scenes from it. He always did that before a picture. I guess a lot of actors do. Charlie was very disarming in that way, because he would shake his head and say, well . . . and then he performed the entire scene. You can imagine how hostesses and guests loved this kind of show. You heard Chaplin, absolutely genuine, no strings attached, giving a performance of himself. He really worked on his performances in public—quite often.

On *Madame Curie,* his first film, Aldous got very turned on by all that material. He was studying up on it. He really loved researching, you know.

[Aldous] was good friends with George Cukor [director of *Madame Curie*]. George—what a charmer! Cukor was certainly not the very slightest bit illiterate in any sense of the word. Everybody was doubtless being a bit tactful. Aldous, you see, was not quite the sort of dreamy angel cruising just above the rooftops. He knew one end of the stick from the other, all right. He'd seen a good deal of life in all sorts of circumstances.

Aldous was shy in an English way, and I could cope with that, of course. I can do all that stuff. We got along splendidly. As a matter of fact, Maria was adorable, too. She was a very gossipy person, and she took an enormous interest in all of their friends, this, that, and the other. I used to tell her the most indiscreet things about myself.

They rediscovered California for themselves. They said it was absolutely beautiful, magnificent. Californians were quite moved to tears, some of them, by being told California was beautiful because Aldous simply couldn't help it—he took such an interest in it that the next thing you knew, he knew everything about it. So he became really quite an expert on California. He used to say that he just picked up information everywhere. He read the newspapers. He read everything he could lay hands on. He read fantastically. He found all kinds of reading interesting. I suppose it was really the curiosity which he had in his blood, of the very great scientist.

Jacob Zeitlin (bookseller and literary agent)

Walter Wanger called me and said, "Mr. Hearst wants to publish a series of letters by prominent writers of the world condemning Hitler. Do you think that Aldous Huxley would write one?" So I asked him, and he wrote me a letter in which he explained why he wouldn't.[9] I didn't approve of [his position]. Aldous said that indignation was a very pleasant emotion, but it was no substitute for doing anything; and the cure for Nazism lay in trying to change the essential morality of the individuals involved, and that he felt that to express his indignation or to write letters to the press would be like putting a plaster on a smallpox pustule. It was not getting at the seat of the disease.

I said that I felt he was mistaken, that he still had an obligation to express himself. As I remember, I said that silence could often be interpreted as approval.

Aldous believed in passive resistance. It's a curious thing; while he believed in passive resistance, I remember their friends Frieda and D. H. Lawrence were very abusive and critical of Bertrand Russell for going to jail as a war resister in World War I.

Aldous did join in a protest with PEN in the 1950s, the international writers group. His basic belief was that the causes of war were too deep to be dealt with by direct confrontation. He felt that, as [Mortimer] Alder put it, the murdered one is also guilty. It was he who first expressed to me the idea that we are responsible for whatever happens to us. Whether it's an accident, or what we think is an accident, that somewhere in back of it lies a conscious decision. We decide to do something or not to do something.

Remember this: in many ways, Aldous was cut off from the world because of his blindness. I think he thought of a great many things in generalities rather than in specific instances of the individual caught, for instance, in a Nazi concentration camp.

Huxley's curiosity led him to explore an aspect of Californian health culture crucial to achieving a lifelong ambition—improving his sight. Especially appealing were the eye exercises of Dr. W. H. Bates, whose book *How to Improve Your Eyesight* became a sort of gospel for him. Huxley's active discovery of the Bates method coincided with his studies of Hinduism under Swami Prabhavananda (alongside Heard and Isherwood). In the 1940s, war news from Europe plunged Aldous and Maria into depression, because of the failure of pacifists to force a diplomatic solution and because of the fate of friends and family left behind. Feelings of impotence at the turn of historical events may have accentuated Huxley's attention to visual self-help, where something tangible might be achieved.

Eyewitnesses disagree about the results of Huxley's eye exercises: some say his sight increased dramatically; others that he deluded himself as to the method's effectiveness. Few understood exactly how poor Huxley's vision had been previously. Few also realized how convinced Huxley was that he was losing what little visual acuity he had. "By 1937, he was more and more worried about losing his sight entirely," Matthew Huxley recalls.

Huxley wrote his explanation of and appreciation for the Bates method in *The Art of Seeing,* 1942. A comparison with Bates's own writings suggests that there may be more of Huxley than of Bates's theory in this work. Sections on visual retraining are mixed with meditation and Hindu mysticism to reach the goal of seeing clearly. Throughout the later part of his life, Huxley struggled to "see" beyond his considerable physical handicap; the quest would eventually lead him to experiment with hallucinogens and parapsychology.

Peggy Kiskadden (friend)

I don't think Aldous ever realized it was his extraordinary memory that was working in the Bates [method]. It wasn't really anything going back-and-forth with the eyes—this wasn't really improving his eyesight at all; but I think that he was so anxious to make it help because he longed so for better vision that actually he was granted better vision. This sounds perhaps ridiculous, but I mean that he learned to use every bit of memory; for instance, if you drove somewhere with Aldous, he always knew where you should turn, and I would say, "Aldous, I can't remember, do we turn left at Highway something?" He would know.

Aldous may have written [in] longhand, but I think mostly on the typewriter. It was a special typewriter [with large letters]. It was the sort of thing you took care not to look at too closely because you never wanted him to feel that you were being intrusive; I never wanted him to think that I noticed that he didn't see well.

He wouldn't say anything, but you'd know you had intruded. Usually you just walked quite close to him, waited, and went across. He moved with you. I never took his arm. I felt somehow that he'd rather be independent.

Jacob Zeitlin (bookseller and literary agent)
Huxley tried all kinds of [ocular remedies]—the Bates method. I don't know how he was prevailed on not to do more of that, but by that time, he had very little eyesight left. He had one small opening in one eye that he could see with, [but] he could see more than you or I [could] with our good eyes. He believed the Bates method really helped, but in my opinion, I don't think it did. You see, he discarded his glasses; [but] his glasses weren't helping him much anyway. He was beyond their help.

Jeanne Neveux (sister-in-law)
He heard of Mrs. Corbett [a teacher of the Bates method in L.A.] and his eyes were getting worse and worse when they were in America, suddenly. Maria wrote and said that Aldous was going to meet this woman that is going to be extraordinary. Of course, it was. He left off his glasses. He's reading, and he's doing something—and it's not for the sake of showing how well he can do things without glasses.

Even the looks of his eyes changed, although one eye was blurred. The blue was not perfectly blue; it was sort of whitish, and the eye didn't look that well. The other eye was brighter and he could see more without his [glasses] than he ever saw with them. She did marvelous things, but it took a long, long time. He used to go see Mrs. Corbett, and it lasted over an hour and a half, each session, and he went every day. Bates offered good use of the eyes, having the eyes move when you look around. Aldous got up and pushed his head forward, straining his neck. Oh, it changed his life. He could use his eyes better. You could always see him palming.

If it was a beautiful bright day and he was going out and walking and he had time, he would sit down on a bench and take the sun on his eyes. It's a terrible strain, not seeing and using your eyes badly.

Aldous was so pleased when I went over to take up Bates training in London. I owe all my life to them because it was just after the war here, my husband was not doing well, although we had this huge flat, and they paid for my stay in London, paid for the teaching.

In the beginning his eyesight was absolutely awful. Well, he couldn't see; he stooped, you know? He was very tall and his head was down. He had special glasses to look at things and double glasses; he had a typewriter [with large letters]. When his eyes were better, he used a normal typewriter. It was just a problem all the time, Aldous's eyes, and "Aldous is tired." I think it [writing] gave him headaches. He didn't know that covering his eyes would rest them; he knew nothing.

Lawrence Powell (librarian)

I cataloged the D. H. Lawrence manuscripts for Frieda. That's how I met Aldous. I was out of library school looking for a library job. There weren't any. So, Zeitlin came back [from the Lawrence Ranch] carrying Aldous Huxley on the end of the rope, dragging him into Hollywood to earn a few bucks. Jake persuaded Aldous Huxley to write the introduction to [a catalog of Lawrence's manuscripts]. I met Huxley in Jake's shop. That's where you met everybody. It was the Grand Central Station of L.A. [for European intellectuals].

Huxley was tall; I'm sure I came up about to his belt

buckle. He talked in this wonderful high, bell-like English voice—fluty, way up high. That impression [remained], and his almost bird-like alertness. He was always looking around and picking up on everything. Very sensitive receptors.

Jacob Zeitlin (bookseller and literary agent)

At the time of the Stalin-Hitler pact, the attack on Poland took place. Aldous didn't see it: he went into a—he isolated himself. There was one man who worked for a bookseller and afterwards became a story editor at Warner Brothers. I remember his telling me in detail how Aldous had called him up and asked him to come over, and he was in tears. He was devastated by what was happening. He was completely out of his mind with it all.

There was always an irrational side to Aldous, as rational as he was. That's why he was so much taken with D. H. Lawrence. D. H. Lawrence had peculiar notions. For instance, Lawrence wrote a series of letters to Bertrand Russell telling him he was a fool for going to jail as a conscientious objector. He railed at him, treated him as if he was an idiot. There was some of that influence; he had such a great reverence for Lawrence and Lawrence represented the anti-rational.

Aldous was disassociated from a lot of the real world. It's astonishing. Partly his blindness, partly losing his mother and then his brother committing suicide—all isolated him. I don't think he lived an idealized life, [but] he was protected by Maria—she took care of the practical parts of his life. He was like a child in many ways. I remember in one of his letters he tells of going away somewhere on a trip, and he and Maria took their most valuable papers down to the filling station at the corner where the man had a safe, and left them with him. For all the great rational machinery, he was in some ways not prepared and not fitted to judge questions like involvement in a war.

He would never have taken part in an organized political party activity. He was apolitical in the sense that he believed—I think he believed—that all politicians were corrupt, that they were motivated by the desire for power. He felt all politicians were inherently corrupt and they were also ideologues; they put the ends above the means and would resort to any means in order to gain their politically desirable ends.

Peggy Kiskadden (friend)

I recall when Aldous was working on *Grey Eminence* in 1940. It was his first biography, and I think it's one of the best books he ever wrote. He was terribly happy because he was using the UCLA library, and he was digging into all kind of memoirs of that period and getting quite a sense of the world at that time and was fascinated by this. It was [at] the same time he was going to Mrs. Corbett and had great hopes of seeing better, so he was in a very good mood.

He loved burrowing into the historical seeing of Père Joseph, and spending hours in the library just fascinated him. There he was with his little glass and utterly happy. That was the world he really fit into. He only did the movie thing out of a curiosity.

In 1941, we went out and lunched with them [at Llano], and then we went out on a walk. We came back across the field, the four of us. It was very sunny, and an old man came toward us and said, "The Japanese have bombed Pearl Harbor." And we all stood there and looked at each other and said, "It's war." Aldous just went blank. Maria said, "Oh, God." Immediately she thought of her family. It's just framed in a picture to me—Maria and Aldous and Bill [Kiskadden] and me walking across the field and hearing that it had started.

Aldous knew it was inevitable; he had worked so hard with the Fellowship of Reconciliation that he was very discouraged about the inevitability of war. Everything that happened he knew would happen.

Chapter III
Llano and Wrightwood (1941–1949)

The U.S. entry into World War II dimmed Huxley's film career, but Huxley had already distanced himself, figuratively and literally, from the film colony. In the months before the Japanese attack, the Huxleys decided to move out of Los Angeles to a quieter, cleaner spot: the shipbuilding industry and other war-related-manufacturing had darkened L.A.'s vistas. As 1941 ended, they bought a tiny farmhouse in the Antelope Valley, north of L.A., and moved in soon after the attack on Pearl Harbor.

The reasons they gave friends and family for the move was that clean desert air would help Huxley's weak lungs, and the bright sun would aid him in the eye exercises with which he persisted, even though it meant Maria had to drive 100 miles round-trip for his appointments. Yet something else must have motivated this self-exile of Huxley's: he was just finishing his great biography, *Grey Eminence,* the story of a seventeenth-century French priest who becomes overinvolved in worldly affairs and was spirituality corrupted. Huxley's studies with the Vedanta Society of southern California had taken him into the realm of mysticism, and he was ever more serious about his meditations. Out of this combination of hermitage and spiritual deepening came *The Perennial Philoso-*

phy, an effort to combine in an anthology what Huxley perceived as unifying substance of the world's religions: mysticism. Thus the war years were the making of yet another side to Huxley: the Stylite, isolated in the desert (where he soon became even more isolated due to wartime tire and gas rationing). Few of his former friends braved the long drive.

These years produced not only *The Perennial Philosophy* but also two parallel works: a novel of human corruption, *Time Must Have a Stop,* and his book on the Bates method, *Art of Seeing.* Each in its way treated the same topics— transcendence and vision. For the first time he made explicit his connection between sight and insight, asserting that through meditation and mysticism, humans could see beyond their limits.

Some said that Huxley had no business sitting out the war in the desert. There were references to Huxley, Isherwood, and others as shirkers in British newspapers. Too old for military service and ineligible because of his eyes, Huxley did not suffer directly, except in the form of declining sales of his works in Britain. Yet one senses in *Perennial* and in the letters Maria wrote to her family in Europe a desire to leave behind a world mired in the present, a world waging a war Huxley believed *could* have been avoided. As Huxley wrote in *The Perennial Philosophy:*

"For they were convinced that Puffing Billy [a train; also a symbol of industrial progress] was hauling them at full speed toward universal peace and the brotherhood of man ... the guarantee that liberty and reason would soon be everywhere triumphant. Puffing Billy has now turned into a four-motored bomber loaded with white phosphorus and high explosives, and the free press is everywhere the servant of its advertisers, of a pressure group, or of the government."[1]

Peggy Kiskadden (friend)

Llano is beautiful country. There are mountains that go off to the right, and you look off over the Mojave Desert.

Where they were was fairly high and very, very healthy for Aldous. They moved out there on account of Aldous, really.

They always drove around a great deal, and they found this old farmhouse where some old people were living and wanted to sell. They bought it and then built a house for Aldous on the land where he could work. It was a charming place.

Across, there was a big range of mountains. There was a great gradual slope onto the Mojave Desert from the San Gabriel mountains on their north side. They had fairly level ground. There was a big field at the back which was left fallow always—just the hay cut from it, and then the house and the little garden. It was just a very simple farmhouse. It was nothing that you looked at twice, but convenient enough.

Aldous's house was lovely, big enough so that he had a big studio and a desk with a view out over the Mojave. What more does a writer want? Plenty of windows.

I think they thought the desert air would be awfully good for Aldous. I must say he looked wonderful during those years. He seemed more robust whenever we went out. He looked much healthier. I think he was more at peace during that time than any time I knew him. He loved working on *The Perennial Philosophy*. He read enormously the people he quotes in it, and he knew what he was writing about and it mattered to him very, very much. As for his other books, every time they'd bring one over, Maria would say, "But Peggy, it isn't quite right, is it?" And I'd say, "No, it isn't quite, but it's getting there." She could love him as much as she did and yet retain that sharp, critical [view]. What she meant was not his literary style at all—which was always perfection: she knew he had further to go.

They made out very well, you know, as Americans. They were the greatest friends with all the ranchers who live [in Llano] in the Antelope Valley. Aldous knew absolutely everything about crops—all their business and everything.

Maria seemed to like Llano. And so did Aldous. I saw a

wonderful picture of Aldous treading the grapes out there. A neighbor had the vines and had the big vat. There was Aldous with his trousers rolled up, with a delighted smile on his face treading the grapes in the good, old-fashioned way. He simply loved that. Aldous learned to drive in Llano. There were dirt roads and lots of uninhabited places. Maria told me about it, with her eyes dancing. It meant a lot to Aldous, who had always been driven everywhere.

They thought the Bates system and Mrs. Corbett, out here in L.A., helped enormously. I think that it did help him to use what sight he had and to use any other ways of perception. I don't think it cleared anything in the eye at all; of course, it didn't change the condition.

Ellen Hovde (daughter-in-law)

Aldous could husband his resources when he needed them. He could see very little in dim light. He would introduce himself to you in a dim room because he didn't know who you were if there were a lot of people around.

[Yet] he could win at a game of ring toss because he could direct his vision for a specific purpose. I think he probably tired quickly. He wore pinhole glasses to read because it kind of concentrated his vision. He did Bates exercises every day.

I think the exercises probably did help. What can one say about his vision? Going through a museum with him was wild because he would gallop. I would read the labels. He had a magnifying glass and he would go over the painting like that, and then we'd go on. We went through it lickety-split, and then he would discourse for four hours on the paintings afterwards because he'd seen everything and noticed everything.

He would do terrible things. He fell over a stool in a motel one night and had a goose egg on his shin, just enormous, because he simply didn't see that kind of thing and he was in a strange room.

Siggy Wessberg (nephew-in-law)

I did the Bates method too, for a while, the same method that [Aldous used] because I'm nearsighted. I had done the palming. He used to do that a lot, and for a while we would sit there. While we were talking, he'd take the palm of his hand and stick it right in his eyelid, almost crunch it up. Back then I used to have more migraines, and I tried it. It did help. Then I did the Bates method for a while, but you have to stick with it.

Apparently it saved him, or did a lot for him. You were never really aware that he was blind unless you looked at him, and you could see one eye was sort of glassy.

Even after he moved out to the desert, Huxley kept up his ties to the film studios, which were providing him sustenance when his British royalties were frozen because of the war. In 1940, he had completed *Pride and Prejudice*. In 1943, he was called to Twentieth Century-Fox to adapt *Jane Eyre* for the screen, under the direction of Darryl Zanuck and in the stimulating company of Orson Welles and noted playwright John Houseman. The Huxleys would drive into town for a few days at a time, having rented a pied-à-terre at the edge of Beverly Hills, then return to Llano. Unfortunately for Huxley, the studios were under growing pressure from the government to turn out win-the-war films; projects on which Huxley was uninterested (and probably unwanted). The Federal Bureau of Investigation began tracking Huxley because of his reputation as a pacifist.[2] Huxley's other anti-war friends, such as Greta Garbo, also left the film world at this time.

In this period, Huxley found himself increasingly isolated, not just from town life, but from his friends. Isherwood was working with the Quakers in Pennsylvania, Gerald Heard had moved into the Laguna Hills to set up a monastery, just after the two friends had drifted apart, according to Peggy Kiskadden and Maria's letters to her sisters.[3]

At the period when Huxley and his best friend had their

worst falling out, and were the most physically separated since they'd all come to California—Laguna was fifty miles south of L.A. and the Huxleys' home in the Mojave, ninety miles north—their intellectual exchange persisted, as each separately pursued in fiction and essay the same topics (which would reoccur as leitmotifs in their writings of the 1940s and '50s): the transcendental, mystical moment; after-life (or after-death) experience; and the use of science fiction to explore the contemporary trends worrying the two—overpopulation, rearmament, and the lack of spiritual understanding in the culture as a whole.

Another part of this isolation was the criticism Isherwood, Auden, and Huxley received from England, where some accused them of sitting out the war in the sybaritic comforts of southern California.

Christopher Isherwood (friend, coauthor)

I think the films he worked on bothered him. I think he found it harder [as time went on]. It embarrassed him somehow, I always felt. I say this with total authority because I not only worked with him, but we were intent on earning our livings. We always got interested, of course; the only real side of total "no-goodness" is when you aren't interested in your work. That's really the end. Then one should leave.

There might have been a period when Aldous felt embarrassed for a while, but I think he could live with it. You see, wise, braver, nobler people than any of us were doing it, and hating it far more than we did. They weren't miserable fools, these people in the studios. They knew what Aldous was worth, and they knew how Aldous could best serve them. They hit on things that interested Aldous.

Aldous was not in the very least bit superior. He, who seemed like the most elevated being in some ways, was nevertheless perfectly charming. The neighbors would come when they were in their little house near the mountains. They would start talking about all kinds of things to do with wildlife, and crops, and problems—Aldous just as much or more than any of them. He was extraordinary!

[In England during the war] there were attacks in the press, particularly on Auden and on me, I think, and on a few others. I'm perfectly well aware that some people said we ran away, but you know, I don't look at it like that because my whole life was running away from England.

Naomi Mitchison (friend)

We knew that he'd gone to Hollywood hoping to get a film done. We were all rather sorry for him because he was always having things promised and nothing coming of them. It seemed such a miserable kind of life—just hanging around there and . . . I didn't feel he'd run away. Nor did I feel that about the other people who went, like W. H. Auden.

We realized by that time how very badly both the army and the people at home had been treated during the first war—how they'd been lied to, and how bad the generals had been.

Peggy Kiskadden (friend)

During the war, Gerald and Aldous realized that a close relationship wasn't going to go on, because Aldous was ever so much more catholic in his interests and tastes, and in his knowledge of music and of various disciplines. Gerald was much more concerned with the life of the spirit. Yet even when the fire came [in 1961]—much later, after Maria had died and they lost everything they had—it was to Gerald that Aldous went. Laura went to Mrs. Virginia Pfeiffer [her longtime friend]. There was a very deep friendship between Aldous and Gerald, but they went their separate ways because of quite different approaches to life.

Mary Anita Loos (friend)

At Christmas, we used to go out to Pearblossom [near Llano] where the Huxleys had their little place. One Christmas my father [Clifford Loos, Anita's brother] said, "I wonder what in God's name we're going to have for dinner." We knew it wouldn't be turkey and cranberry sauce.

When we got there, Maria said, "I've just done something wonderful for dinner. Somebody said you should roast a chicken for an hour. I decided if you did it slowly for five hours it would be better."

Well, you can imagine—it was like eating jerky. Then she said, "I have something really marvelous. I have big, beautiful baked potatoes." My father loved baked potatoes, and he said, "Well, that's great." Maria said, "I baked them in the earth; I hear they're better that way. So we ate them with bits of dust stuck to the skins."

Betty Wendel (friend)

[How much was he in touch with what was going on in Europe?] Maria read the newspapers to him, and he listened to the radio all the time. He wanted to be away from the war, possibly because he couldn't be part of it. He wouldn't have fought because he was a pacifist, but he wanted to get away from it all.

Lawrence Powell (librarian)

In 1943, Huxley gave a public lecture at UCLA in Royce Hall; he was such a persuasive speaker, I think by his simplicity. He came through as a very simple person, his public image, yet his whole mind was full of wheels and mechanisms that were turning, but he came out in a simple flow and the students hung on him. I became head librarian the next year, in '44, and he depended on us for books that we could get for him.

Generally he'd come to my office. I closed my official administrative office at five in the afternoon. He'd show up then, because the phone didn't ring and there was nobody else. He'd come in bringing books back and say, "Larry, why don't you get me these," and leave me a list.

He used the catalog a great deal. He was so conspicuous

because of his height and his semi-blindness, and he'd get a card catalog tray and bring it out and hold the whole goddamn tray up to his face. Students wondered, "Jesus, what is that man doing?" They didn't realize he was blind. And he had to look at things very close.

They began to follow him. Students would trail him and ask questions because they knew he'd respond. He'd never talk down or never turn away anyone. That's why they loved him. He was interested; he wanted to know what they thought, what they wanted, what they were thinking of. Full of curiosity.

To Aldous, libraries were like food, they fed him.

Rose D'Haulleville (sister-in-law)

Huxley was very interested in religions. We [the Nys family] were Catholic—he told me one time, "You know, if I had to choose a religion, I would choose Catholicism." He admired Catholicism very much. It was a main interest.

I was talking with Krishnamurti in Wrightwood. He and Huxley were walking between the trees and talking and discussing, and all of a sudden a rain of stones and things were thrown at them. They turned around and went back on the safe road and into the village and asked, "Who belongs to that land?" "Oh," they said, "that belongs to a convent, and it was the nuns that were keeping you two out of their property."

I couldn't believe that even here, in Llano, when he was talking to the workmen, or in a garage or anywhere, the way Aldous would talk to the people. Aldous was interested in the working class, the working people, and how they think, and how they were working. I imagine that when he'd meet people like that, he'd talk about their job and ask questions—he was curious; he wanted to know things.

During the war years, Huxley worked more or less simultaneously on three books, which catalog his interests of those lonely years: *The Art of Seeing* (1942), an autobiographical account of his visual difficulties; *Time Must Have a Stop* (1944), a novel; and *The Perennial Philosophy* (1945), his ambitious effort to find in mysticism a common ground among the world's religions. His readings in Hinduism and in Christian mysticism left him serene and grounded in the sort of genteel rural poverty some of his Bloomsbury circle had sought.

In one of the more bizarre episodes in Huxley's life, at the moment when he was arguably most at peace (in the middle of war), he was banished from his desert refuge—by a rash. Huxley never was terribly healthy; in fact, some might depict him as a mild hypochondriac, because his physical illnesses coincided with personal and writing crises.

In any case, whether the culprit was an elm tree (as Maria's sister Rose insists) or the tiny horehound plant, as others claim, Huxley could no longer tolerate life in Llano. Rather than return to the city, however, the family decided to move to a higher elevation in Wrightwood (which later became a ski resort). Just as the hero of his postwar novel *Ape and Essence* disappeared from his desert home, Huxley was driven by health from his garden of content.

Rose D'Haulleville (sister-in-law)

Aldous had a lot of doctors, dentists, and all his jobs were in Los Angeles. They had to drive so much back and forth [from Llano to L.A.] that it got very tiresome, especially for Maria. Maria was very delicate. She was strong, in a way, but she was not a big, tough woman. She was slender and skinny and took good care of herself—not so much for herself, but to be in good health for Aldous.

Aldous developed an allergy. He had been working in the garden. They didn't go directly to Los Angeles. They picked all the things he touched in the garden and analyzed them to find out. He had this terrible rash and swelling in his face so that he could hardly open his eyes anymore. It was just a big tree, the elm.

Amazingly so, because I've never heard before or since

that an elm tree could cause rashes. He developed this rash whenever he'd go in the garden; and he'd wait awhile [in L.A.] and then he'd come back, of course. They had [the garden] in the back of the house; it doesn't exist anymore. There was an apple orchard there and they had vineyards— they even made grapes.

Already, probably, they thought it was time they moved, but they went much further up. They went to Wrightwood, in the San Gabriel mountains. You go into Wrightwood, and then you arrive in the big place where the shops are. You stay on the road that goes toward Big Pine and it was, at that time, the house before the last one, in Wrightwood. In the last house, the people were raising foxes—poor Aldous and Maria. I think they left Wrightwood because of the smell of the foxes. It was terribly strong.

It was a very small house, smaller than the one in Llano and not really very interesting or pretty. Aldous worked in a trailer in back. He always had to isolate himself.

Peggy Kiskadden (friend)

Llano was desert, great vistas of desert with the air trembling over it. Wrightwood was full of trees; it was higher, you see. That's why they got it, because when it got very hot in Llano it was a good place to go. It wasn't too far a drive from Llano to Wrightwood. Wrightwood was dark with trees all around, and they planned to build a house on one of these lots that they bought, and that we would build a house there. But that never transpired. It must have been that the allergies [he had] made them turn off from Llano and think that Wrightwood, being higher and more mountainous, would be better for him.

She [Maria] loved Llano, so I can imagine it was [a sense of loss]. I know that when we went up to Wrightwood with them—we met them up there, and they were showing us the lots that they had bought and which lot they thought we should buy. We did buy it. When we did, Maria said, "Oh, thank God!" It mattered very much to her to have a little support. She was always thinking, "What if Aldous is ill, I couldn't leave him to go for help."

I think the war darkened Aldous's feelings anyway, and the end of the war wasn't going to solve everything. When Russia took over the eastern provinces, one knew there was going to be trouble. That was always in the back [of his mind] as a kind of sadness. It was just a different world, after the Second World War.

[When in town] he would write all morning, and [Igor] Stravinsky would compose all morning. Then we'd all meet at the Farmers Market around one-thirty or two and have lunch. They were both solitary workers.

It would be a long lunch, about an hour and a half. It was a time for them to relax. Aldous always loved talking to Stravinsky, and Stravinsky loved him. They had a wonderful relationship because Aldous knew a great deal about music.

In 1948, Stravinsky looked more like an insect than anything. He was almost bald, and he had a narrow head. Their relationship was [close] because Aldous knew things Stravinsky didn't, and Stravinsky knew things Aldous didn't. So they were both terribly anxious to get at what the other knew. That was what made a most lovely relationship. When it came to *The Rake's Progress,* it was Aldous who suggested that W. H. Auden [do the libretto]. They had a wonderful working relationship because it never impinged one on the other, but augmented [each] in a very nice way.

[In Los Angeles] we used to have concerts that were called "Evenings on the Roof." Stravinsky would sit there in the front row with music in front of him, and Aldous would almost always sit quite close to him. Aldous had a great feeling about music, and he wanted to know how it felt to be a musician. He was the same way about art.

I'll never forget taking him to the museum. He had his little glass that he always had, and he read the pictures, back and forth, like this, and I stood there. I couldn't keep the tears back. It was so terrible, that this man who loved art, who wrote about art, who did that lovely book on the [Piranesi] etchings, and this is how he had to see.

That was quite early on, and I think that's what really cemented my love for Aldous. I thought that he cared enough about it so that even if he had to take it *in seriatim*, he did it. How many people would just have said, "I can't see"?

There was something about Aldous that was terribly touching if you happened to catch him. Otherwise, he was quite aloof and always spoke in this voice that was so detached. When you saw him do a thing like this and heard him breathing fast because he was so excited, all of a sudden you got within and realized, "This is not only a person who knows how to use words, he's a totally adorable person."

Ellen Hovde (daughter-in-law)

[What did he do for fun?] He liked shopping for food in the supermarket. I don't think he had any real things that he did except when he wasn't working. He liked observing or having experiences or going places, and we used to drive around a lot and look. He liked meeting people who weren't like him, and people who weren't afraid of him, so they would just talk. He loved talking to women who were chatty. He liked that very much. In fact, he loved Paulette Goddard—one of his favorite persons in the world.

I remember a party at Anita Loos's and she was wearing a short, rainbow-lamé, shiny dress. He thought she was smashing. She was very bright, too, and very funny, and had that kind of iconoclastic quality which he adored.

After the war ended, Huxley's finances were in a shambles, which once again inspired hopes of having films made from his writings. He and Burgess Meredith hoped to film *Brave New World*, to be acted in (and financed by) Paulette Goddard. The project was abandoned when RKO refused to release the rights Huxley's British agent sold for a pittance some years before. Huxley did write a telling preface to a new edition, which reveals many of his preoccupations in the postwar years. He then drafted screenplays with friends such as Isherwood and the director Zoltan Korda—to little avail. (One of the last film projects that captivated him was an adaptation of *Alice in Wonderland,* on which he worked for Walt Disney.) In 1948, the first film made from his work, *A Woman's Vengeance,* was finally shown but received little critical acclaim. Huxley's career as a screenwriter was ending; his avocation as a seer had begun.

The reasons Huxley ceased to obtain sought-after film-writing commissions are obscure: was it, as his agent's wife Dorris Halsey suspected, because his language was "too good" for Hollywood, attributing this reluctance to work with Huxley to the declining literacy among top producers? Yet the producers with whom Huxley worked, such as George Cukor or Zoltan Korda, were anything but illiterate.

Another possible explanation is that as the wartime influx of European directors and producers reversed, those who remembered Huxley as a scandalous, best-selling author no longer held sway in the studios. A third possibility is that because he had made himself unavailable for win-the-war films—and was attacked publicly as a shirker by British film producers such as Michael Balcon, Huxley's reputation as a scriptwriter was tainted by charges of unpatriotism, in a lordly patriotic era.

In any case, the key writings from Huxley's postwar period (particularly *Science, Liberty and Peace,* and *Ape and Essence*) form two strikingly different yet parallel revisions of Huxley's credo on science. *The Gioconda Smile,* also from this period, similarly suggests a period of disaffection and cynicism.

Burgess Meredith (actor)

When we worked together in L.A., as we did maybe three or four times, it consisted of my asking questions (which Huxley liked) as to a possible rewriting of certain other alternatives that *Brave New World* might offer. He juggled the thoughts, and said, "No, I believe this." And, "This would be possible." He'd think about it and so on, and he made notes. Now, I jump to the fact that he called and he said to please come over; he had some rather bad news. He found that he couldn't fool with it—some "shyster" lawyer had. . . . He was pretty bitter about it. I remember he used some surprising, angry words—somebody had taken his rights and he had no right to write on it anymore for a movie.

We were talking about how an up-to-date *Brave New World* might work and in the process, we got to talking about hypnosis. We saw each other and enjoyed talking with each other and Paulette, too (though she was in a film during most of this). He made notes, and I made many suggestions and, if you remember, in the later edition of *Brave New World*, he spoke of those days. I remember that I brought up questions of, "Would you really write it this way today?"

Paulette [who was married at this time to Meredith] was extremely beautiful and sexy—bright and funny and civilized—she was at her very top. Certainly, I would never have had that kind of access to him; he enjoyed being around her, and I think he remembered her with Chaplin. She had great flirtations with him; I wouldn't be surprised if [an affair] had happened, because she did with many people, but as to a serious affair, I never heard it. After we broke up, they might have had some further flirtation, but I'm saying I can't say.

Two periods of our relationship are worth noting: both occurred generally at our apartment [while Aldous was over] for dinner or supper, something like that. The first was the recasting of *Brave New World;* the second was our experimentation with hypnosis in which several people were brought up and put under hypnosis by this doctor.

The conversation went something like this: Huxley said, "Could you see how he would respond? (He [the subject] talked as though he couldn't hear you when he was told to.)

"Could you see how he responds if he moves into the future?" And the doctor did so.

"Where are you now?" and he said, "I'm sitting here in the living room." All of a sudden he said, "Do you think you can go forward in time?" to the man. Well, I was fascinated, and so was Huxley. So, the conversation went: "I want you now to get on the river of time, and on the river of time, you're not going back"—I know this man used the river of time; we were rowing back and forth or something, I don't know—and he said, "You're going forward, you're going forward up the river of time, and I want you to look around you and find out what date it is." And the man said something like "1952."

The doctor asked him, "What are you doing?" and he said, "I'm reading the funny papers." That got the hypnotist, he didn't know what to make of it. He said, "Never mind about that, what's on the front page?" And he said, "Nothing much on the front page except the assassination of [sic] President Wallace" (who was vice president at that time).

Jacob Zeitlin (bookseller and literary agent)

Matthew would very quickly challenge Aldous. He was like a lot of sons are; they want to put the old man down, and so there was a lot of debate between them. There got to be a time when Matthew was very hostile to Maria, and he and Aldous became very much closer. I think that they all went to a counselor to discuss the problem.

Matthew felt that Maria had abandoned him. He felt that being sent off to school meant they didn't want him; he felt rejected. They had quite a lot of working out to do over that. Aldous stepped in and sort of realized that Matthew needed him, that he needed to communicate with Matthew more. They established a bond which I don't think they had before.

He was totally uninvolved with matters like labor disputes until his own son got into a dispute out at Warner Brothers

Studio and was walking in a picket line and was knocked down by a fire hose. Aldous picketed, too.

Matthew was working at the studios [Warner Brothers] as a reader. The readers all went on strike along with [the Conference of Studio Unions]. They picketed the studio and the studio hired a bunch of goons and also had the firemen turn the fire hose on them.

Laura Huxley (writer, second wife)

In Hollywood if you want to make a package, you need a writer and a director, and then you get a star. I had just met John Huston, because I had asked him to speak for a film that was a benefit for the Italian orphans a couple years before the 1945 film *Open City*, by [Roberto] Rossellini. I had presented it here, and John Huston had come. He was one director that I knew. Somebody said to me, "You need a writer," and I said, "Well, who is a good writer?" They said, "Well, there is this writer, Huxley." I said, "I heard about this man who is speaking of babies in bottles; is that the same fellow?" They said, "Well, yes. He lives in California." I said, "Well, what is his address?" So somebody gave me his address, and I just wrote him: "I have to come and see you because I have a wonderful idea for a film."

My temper has always been very quick; so when two days passed, then three days passed, and he still hadn't answered me, I thought, "What's this!?" So I called him up and they told me then there was no telephone in his house, and they called him at the post office like it was very urgent and I said, "This is important. I am going to Italy. I have to see you right away," and Aldous said, "Well, come tomorrow then," and so I met these lovely, lovely, people.

After eleven years in the United States, in 1948 the Huxleys were finally ready to visit Europe. They stayed with Maria's sister Jeanne Neveux in Paris and with Julian and Juliette Huxley in London. Their mood was anything but optimistic: in letters they declared their horror of finding a Europe devastated by war.

Huxley apparently suspected his career as a screenwriter was at an end; after a singular lack of success obtaining assignments from Paramount and other studios, he savaged Louis B. Mayer of MGM, in the introduction to that dark novella, *Ape and Essence* (1948).

As usual, when Huxley suffered a major emotional professional setback, his physical health felt the impact. While writing one of the essays that would be published as *Themes and Variations,* "Variations on a Philosopher," Huxley experienced a severe and prolonged case of bronchitis. This fascinating study of Maine de Biran (like Father Joseph of *Grey Eminence,* a philosopher who mixed in politics) is one of Huxley's best biographies, while simultaneously serving as a catalog of his enthusiasms of the 1950s, particularly mesmerism and parapsychology. This important work shows signs of the cinematic styling (establishing shots, visual cues to characterization) he had learned in the film studios. He began the book after visiting southern France in the late 1940s.

Maria Huxley seriously considered staying on in Europe, according to her letters. Huxley was committed to a return to the United States, having refused to sell their new house in Wrightwood or to consolidate their possessions. Europe did not seem the direction of his future, despite his family ties.

Ellen Hovde (daughter-in-law)

He must have seen his life as a real schism; coming to America was a very different kind of life. He never went back to the other. He went back to visit and look at it, and I think he was incredibly attached to Julian, but they certainly were very different.

Jeanne Neveux (sister-in-law)

When Aldous and Maria came to Paris, Sophie [Neveux] had a boyfriend who had three Bugattis. We were always trying them out to see whether they would go two hundred kilometers an hour; it's fantastic. We took Aldous for a spin. We went in the fastest possible way and he just adored it, because he didn't see the dangers. Maria would have made a very good racer; she was terrific. Speed was something that was a terrific sensation for him. He would say, "Oh, this is absolutely marvelous." It's like a poppy which all at once is open. He had these moments where he had this real enjoyment of things.

Juliette Huxley (sister-in-law)

After World War II, I used to watch their [Julian and Aldous's] relationship, being "in the middle," as it were. It was mostly intellectual. I don't mean to cast a slur on their affection, because they were deeply devoted to each other. *No* doubt. This [affection] mostly took the form of discussing the latest scientific discovery, or, perhaps, a remedy which Aldous was interested in. He was always interested—tremendously interested—in what could *improve* human appreciation, health, or almost anything.

They would come down to breakfast about eighty-thirty, sit around the round table there, and start discussing. They would go on talking until about eleven, and then Julian would jump up [and exclaim], "Oh, my God, I've got to go to my job!" Then Aldous would slowly gather himself together and go to London Library, and he would collect some more books. He had armfuls of books which he read with one eye—amazingly—and sometimes with a magnifying glass. At home, Maria read to him by the hour. She had a special way of reading. She read all in one sentence; she never took any kind of [breath]; she never stressed a phrase. And Aldous sat there, taking it all in. His memory was trained to remember everything. He had to. It was one of the things which was, in a way, a great acquisition, because a person's memory, generally, is not particularly trained; but he had trained his to remember every word read out of a book.

We were in Paris, and they came there. Maria had about

five boxes full of things—presents for her family. Her sister
Jeanne Neveux and Maria were very close, and Maria wrote
wonderful letters.

Julian was director-general of UNESCO—up to his eyes
in work—and really completely embedded. So we saw Aldous and Maria, themselves very much embedded with their
family. Maria was rather disturbed at the time. Frankly, I
think Maria was tired out. She was a frail person; she was
delicate. She drove the car miles and miles—a big car. Aldous had bought her a special car which could be moved
with less effort. She took him to doctors; she took him to
whatever special treatment he had to have. And that was
very often. She did a lot of his letters. She typed his manuscripts. She read to him by the hour. She traveled with him;
she planned; she had parties for him.

When he came to London, I looked after him. In fact—
oh, this is funny—Maria always wrote to me beforehand:
"Aldous is to eat no meat at all, very little milk," a diet. I
took no notice of it. I gave him plenty of meat, which he
liked, plenty of milk, which he didn't mind, and free food—
whatever he liked. He put on ten pounds. That was a
triumph.

If he had turned away from his English background, he
certainly didn't turn away from his brother, because he
came here and stayed the full three weeks planned in their
holiday. They looked to me really close, very happy together.
But again, they never took at each other: never saying, "Jolly
good fellow," or giving each other a playful kick or something. It was all "up here" (points to head).

Peggy Kiskadden (friend)

Aldous was always rather frail. With this great big frame
he was never robust. You knew that if he got overtired, he'd
probably get a cold. He hadn't the resistance that a very
healthy person has. Maria knew that; that's why she took
such beautiful care of him.

[After Europe], I think he was ready to move back to the

city. I think Maria thought they needed to be nearer to doctors; his health was always so fragile. She felt this [was] just too far away to be, and I think they were always restless. They went everywhere and stayed for a while and moved on.

There were some paintings that Aldous had done. There was a painting of Maria. He did a lot of painting at one time. They never collected things.

[When they moved back to L.A.] I don't think they did anything but just put their trunks down full of manuscripts and various gadgets that could make for comfort. They were not particularly interested in visual things. I like a house that you come into and you feel at home; you see things you like to look at. They, after all, had come to this country and left everything, and there was nothing of that, ever, in any place they lived. It was nothing that struck you as being enormously comfortable or cozy.

In the late 1940s, Maria was getting increasingly tired. Yes, I felt that her life was too hard. It was. It was extremely hard. Aldous would be sitting there placidly writing; but she would be coming back and forth to gather supplies, to see to things that had to be seen to.

Francis Huxley (nephew)

My father Julian was an enthusiast for anything that he had learnt. He used to quote Bertrand Russell's remark: "Isn't it fun to *know* things!" quite frequently. He would regale family and acquaintances with facts about the sexual life of giraffes. In fact, I remember one occasion when Aldous came to stay with the family. I arrived at breakfast rather late; they were already in full flow. Julian was talking about the homosexual behavior of adolescent giraffes and, I also think, the digestive habits of rabbits. Instead of chewing their cud, they used to eat their feces the first time 'round— to get the best out of them. The second time 'round, they just let them lie.

Aldous listened to these observations with interest. He always did; he loved scientific details and nonsenses of this kind. And he replied with a story from one of Boccaccio's contemporaries—of a monk who had been proved to be an adulterer. Then he went on to talk of the vision of St. Catherine of Siena, who had been married to Jesus in a dream, and Jesus had put on her ring finger, as a token of the marriage, a ring which was in fact his severed prepuce. Aldous was very fond of those stories. It was part of the late Victorian—well, mostly Edwardian—time in which this kind of storytelling was a good social manner of showing yourself in public.

Julian and Aldous took a walk with the wives following: they were doing this kind of storytelling with each other. They told each other all the information about ectomorphs and saints, and Palomar telescopes and red shifts and evolution—everything—telling each other stories. They returned very well satisfied with each other. On the next day, they went for a walk, but by this time they had run out of their anecdotes, and they had nothing to say. It was the women who provided most of the conversation that day. (My mother says that this is entirely false.)

I have heard something rather like it, I must say, between the two of them, because their conversation together was on this level of exchanging information that had come to them, and of either scabrous or fascinating stories. Indeed, once they had run out of their baggage of stories, they didn't have much in the form of private conversation together.

You know how Aldous is. Several terms of admiration— with the state of the world or of the story—was either "extraordinary" or "phenomenal." He liked that word "phenomenal" very much. That was the only time I ever heard a man pronounce the word in that fashion. It gave the word "phen-om-en-al" a very particular sense of being— "phenomenal."

Chapter IV
Los Angeles (1949–1956)

I n the late 1940s (and throughout the next decade), Aldous Huxley traveled a great deal outside of California; he visited New York City and Europe to restore his reputation and to look for devices and operations that would assist his sight. Accordingly, his interest in alternative medicine and physical/mental therapies rose dramatically. Maria's letters to her sisters often discuss the progress of one or another paranormal health experiments.[1]

In these years, the author was drawn to visionaries and mystics, such as St. Catherine of Siena (whose biography he planned for nearly a decade yet never actually drafted) and the twin biographies of priest Urbain Grandier, burned at the stake as a devil, and of Father Surin, his exorcist.

"Demonology doesn't interest me," Huxley wrote during the war; "only the particular case of Loudun, because it happened to involve a very remarkable man, Father Surin."

Passages of *Devils of Loudun,* as Huxley called his book, reflect Huxley's own seeking after light. Particularly after Huxley's severe but short-term loss of vision in 1951 due to acute iritis, his hunger for physical sight motivated his selection of subjects for his writing as he sought words "like lamps, suddenly illuminating a mind that had been darkened by too much brooding," as Huxley wrote in *Devils.*[2]

Juliette Huxley (sister-in-law)

Aldous had pneumonia; he had iritis, which is a terrible burning of the eyes. At one time when he had that [1951], they thought he would lose his eyesight. He luckily recovered, but it was very painful.

Julian was much less prepared to believe a lot of things that Aldous was prepared to, seeing in them the fringe of something which might lead to a better understanding. Julian found he hadn't the time or the aptitude. Aldous was dead serious. Maria, too, in her time.

Laura Huxley (writer, second wife)

Between 1948 and 1953, I had some contact with the Huxleys. We went to parties together. Sometimes I just went there in the evening.

I had followed the lectures of Ron Hubbard in 1950; I knew about it. There was no church then. You just went to the lectures and got a title or something. No, Scientology came later, in '52 or '53.

One time Hubbard came to the lecture and said, "Yesterday I went to see a famous writer but his sight is completely occluded—that means he could not have access to memories and so on . . ." Evidently, that evening they had visited. I already knew Aldous, and I told him and he laughed and said he [Hubbard] had very capable techniques.

Aldous read that book I spoke about *[Dianetics]*. Gerald Heard had also seen Ron Hubbard, who is an intelligent person, a very capable man. I don't know if I judge from now or from then, but I think he is a good technician, which is very different from being a spiritual man.

Aldous looked frail, and the fact that he was so tall and pale [contributed to that appearance], but he was very strong. He did have a flu one or two weeks a year (of course after the cancer that was a different story), but he wasn't frail. He had an active life. He seldom mentioned being tired. He had very, very little sight, but he used the sight

100 percent; while most of us have normal sight and we use maybe 10 percent.

In 1951, A. L. Kitselman wrote a booklet about E [entelechy] therapy. He had been a famous mathematician and then he evolved a very simple—and in many cases good—technique they call "E." E stands for some kind of an inner knowledge for the examiner. So it is in many therapies: that you do not address the intellectual, present person; you ask that being within you who has knowledge and wants the best for you. You try to bypass reasoning. It worked very well; it is a good therapy. This man was very intelligent. I remember him coming up to the house on Deronda Drive [where Laura and Aldous Huxley lived from 1956 until it burned in May 1961]. Maria liked that E therapy.

Aldous said [his feelings on psychotherapy] many, many times in a very clear way. The Freudians only think about the two ends of the gastrointestinal tract. All the rest they leave out. That the Freudians are very involved with the basement full of little monsters but none with the upper part of the individual which is the being—celestial, inspirational. In other words, he would approach it as he approached anything else—with an approach of the whole, not just a little piece. I think that was extraordinary about Aldous—that he was obviously a specialist because he was a writer, but then he was a generalist [too].

He was just a researcher, and he would see what there was and record the good things and the bad things. I don't think he took any [therapies] as though they were the whole [truth]. He never did that. He was studying whatever would come. He would study about garbage with the same interest that he studied psychotherapy.

Of course, ecology was of great interest to him. Everything was part of a whole. He always realized and wondered and was enchanted by the mystery of the whole. He would be interested in all the little things that surrounded the mystery, what could be known.

Even vitamins and minerals and enzymes. [These]

changed every few months because one or another was more important. One time we were experimenting with niacinamide—that makes you all red. I would take it. You cannot stand to have clothes on, and you get all red. He said I looked like an Etruscan statue. You become very active because it is like a push. We were experimenting with dosage. I cannot take very much. He could take quite a dosage of vitamins without having any side effects.

Francis Huxley (nephew)

When I was little, I visited Aldous [at his house] in King's Road. He had this array of vitamins and seaweed pills, and goodness knows what else—that he was busily taking one after another. This filled me with some disquietude. He was interested in all forms of psychological and spiritual techniques for self-advancement.

Peggy Kiskadden (friend)

Aldous had the weirdest ideas about medicine. He had awful doctors. He had a doctor for years, and at one point I said, "I don't know about this Kolish, Bill." So Bill [a physician] just quietly went to the medical library, and he came home with his eyes open; he said, "That man has the largest file of anyone in the medical association!" I said, "What does a large file mean?" "It means that it's full of complaining letters. That's what it means."

Aldous was terribly interested in anatomy, but he didn't really know [about medicine]. Once, when I came out from town and stopped by, Aldous was obviously very ill. He was in bed; his breathing was raspy. So I went to the phone and called Bill. I said, "Could you stop here on the way home?" Bill came and said, "You know, Aldous, we've got to be careful that this doesn't run into pneumonia. I think you'd better go to the hospital." Aldous meekly said, "All right." We got a competent doctor to look after him. He had very delicate lungs, and he became ill very easily.

Ellen Hovde (daughter-in-law)

I must have [visited the Huxleys in California] in 1952. Maria had already had the first cancer operation [January 1951]. (It was after Matthew and I married [April 1950].) I remember we got a letter from her saying, "I'm an Amazon," and she'd had the breast operation.

I don't know whether he knew she still had cancer. He played games with it anyway. He knew and didn't know ... as cancer patients do ... all the time—they're dying, they're not dying. I remember one dinner that the four of us were having, I think it was in New York, where she and I looked at each other and burst into tears. Neither Matthew nor Aldous were acknowledging the fact that she was dying and didn't want to talk about it at all. Aldous really did not want to talk about it. It was very hard for her, *very* difficult for her because she saw herself as someone who always had to help him.

Maria was so completely concentrated on Aldous that I think Matthew suffered from neglect. In spite of a lot of concern, they just really didn't give him the kind of stability that he desperately needed. And then to be the son of a famous parent is a curse you wouldn't wish on anyone. He couldn't really enter the arena against his dad; it was impossible. Aldous found it much easier to be open with me because I wasn't somebody he had to have a certain kind of relationship with.

As to extrasensory phenomena, Maria would throw herself into the whole thing and maybe have afterthoughts. Mainly, her way of dealing with it was to go with it. I think Aldous also would go with it, but only in his Olympian way. Not that he wouldn't try everything. We used to lunch with Gerald Heard at the Farmers Market. He would start very slowly, and then he would be fired up by his conversation and become incredibly witty and funny. He was always brilliant. He [Gerald] had this wicked joy in being an adviser to boards of directors of industry, and there was a great fondness between him and Aldous; they really enjoyed chinning together—they could have a good time. He was the sort of person Aldous could play intellectual games with.

I thought Stravinsky was a very plain, very charming, down-to-earth man. And Vera [Mrs. Stravinsky] was lovely, really warm, a caring person. I expected Stravinsky to be a monument, and instead he said things like, "Hey, why don't we go to the movies." I think he was a much plainer person than [his biographer] Bob Craft makes out or would like to make out. He was small, and there were so many tall Huxleys.

Laura Huxley (writer, second wife)

In 1951, they were living in the Melrose district [of Los Angeles], and Maria said it had been a terrible, terrible period. (I know only through Maria because I spoke to her right afterwards.) He had an attack of iritis; I think that Sybille Bedford put it down correctly [in *Aldous Huxley*]. He really was suffering.

This hypnotist tried to put him under for pain. The interesting thing is that a professor at UCLA [Leslie LeCron]—with very, very normal methods, nothing ritualistic, put him under. Then Aldous could do it himself. He couldn't sleep; he couldn't work because the pain was so bad. I don't know whether it was the cortisone, or a wrong treatment.

Mrs. Corbett assisted him to see. It saved him; he was going blind. He kept on doing the Bates system. Every Tuesday he went to take his lesson from Mrs. Corbett until she died. The reason that his eyes were so good is because he did what most of us don't do. He applied what he believed. Every day he did some of the Bates system. He read in a specific way which was the correct one. Throughout the day he would do exercises, a few minutes here or there. Then he would listen to people.

Aldous's sight was quite mysterious because, first of all, when I married him, one eye was practically gone, and the other one had very little vision. In certain lights, for instance the light that you are in, he could see pretty well. He would say, "Oh, you look well today," if the light was right. If you were sitting [facing the light] he would see fairly well. For reading, he had those Chinese pinpoint glasses, but not ever otherwise. (There is a special way to wear those. You are to move your head all the time.) He had no [other] glasses at all. He had a spyglass with which he would look at paintings, or in the restaurant or if something was shown to him.

If a complete stranger would come to visit, he would not know them. If a person he knew came, of course he would know the voice. Whether he knew it by voice, or by sight [I don't know]. But he would notice every flower; he would notice every tree. In directions, going around the city (I have absolutely no sense of direction), he was always the one who said, "Now right; now left."

Sidney Field (friend)

Before I met Aldous, I used to go to the little public library here, in Hollywood, and I would see this interesting-looking gentleman who was reading this way, practically with his nose, you know, and thinking, "Gosh, he must have very bad eyesight." I didn't know who he was.

Dorris Halsey (agent)

I remember my most disagreeable memory of Aldous Huxley was attending my first Writers' Guild of America dinner, which was then held still at the Palladium in Hollywood. (I called the president, Alan Rifkin, today to find out when that was, and he zeroed it down to 1952.) George Jessel was master of ceremonies.

Writers are a rowdy bunch, and they had been drinking. Aldous came to the podium, and the light was on the lectern. He looked down and took out very strong glasses, and even with the strong glasses, he had to lean very far forward to read the text. That rowdy bunch of writers started tittering and laughing all over the Palladium. I could've sunk under the table, gladly.[3]

My husband, Reece Halsey [who also represented Faulk-

ner, Sinclair, and Michener at the William Morris Agency],
made several film deals for Aldous: *The Gioconda Smile* at
Universal Studios. He also had him work on, I believe, *Alice
in Wonderland,* at Disney.

These were different worlds. Reece took him to a meeting
with Walt Disney, which apparently was epic, because Disney had no idea who and what Aldous Huxley really was. It
was a story conference, and Reece had the impression of it
being almost on two different planes: the two personalities
were so dissimilar, and while Aldous was forever courte-
ous—the tone was one of noblesse oblige—here was this
man who had made a success out of a mouse. He was a
good man and a kind man and a nice man, but certainly
not on a level with an Aldous Huxley when trying to explain
story points. It was sort of weird.

Huxley's *Gioconda Smile,* if you've read it, has wonderful
dialogue. (As a matter of fact, Laura produced the play here
in L.A.) He didn't write the screenplay; I think it was an
outright sale of the book and then some screenwriters were
put on it for Hollywood purposes. His language was too
good for Hollywood.

Yet during those days you had literate producers; you
were not gearing the scripts to the lowest denominator. You
were not catering to the twelve-year-olds. That was still the
golden age, slightly tarnished nevertheless, of Hollywood.
Aldous was certainly a star writer.

I don't think Aldous would have become enamored by
the type of productions which began to evolve [later]. He
couldn't have been, he was on another plateau. He was
terribly reachable—flesh and blood—but intellectually he
was a giant towering over everybody. And the things that
become a revelation to you or to me were a foregone conclusion to him long ago.

Fifteen years after the Huxleys had migrated to the United
States, their son persuaded them to formalize their affection
for their adopted land by becoming citizens. Aldous and

Maria dutifully filled out forms and sat with the crowds in a downtown office of the U.S. Immigration and Naturalization Service in Los Angeles, accompanied by their friend Betty Wendel. Unfortunately for them, U.S. immigration laws at that time required all applicants, regardless of age, to commit themselves to bearing arms in service of their new country. Anyone objecting to this clause had to declare his or her objection as religious, something a grandson of T. H. Huxley, the man who had coined the term "agnostic," was unlikely to do.

Nearly thirty years before, Aldous Huxley had anticipated such a situation in a short story:

"I have no religion," he answered.

"But surely, sir, you must have some kind of religion."

"Well, if I must, if it's in the Army Regulations, you had better put me down as an Albigensian, or a Bogomile, or, better still, as a Manichean . . ."

"But if . . ." the military representative continued, "if your objection is not religious, may I ask what it is?"

"It is based on a belief that all war is wrong, and that the solidarity of the human race can only be achieved in practice by protesting against war, wherever it appears and in whatever form."[4]

According to the F.B.I. records, Aldous Huxley later submitted a statement explaining his objections to bearing arms—and then withdrew his and Maria's applications when it appeared that those applications would be denied.

Betty Wendel (friend)

Matthew wanted them to become American citizens. He just did. He had served in the army—not in combat, he drove an ambulance or something [in the medical corps]. Because he was an American citizen, he wanted them to become American citizens. They were doing it for Matthew.

At the hearings [in 1953], the mood of the judge was very regretful. Aldous, as you know, was a pacifist. He asked Aldous if he would bear arms to protect the country, and [Aldous] said no, he wouldn't. Would he drive an ambulance? He said yes. (He couldn't drive anywhere!) Maria said exactly what Aldous had said, that she was a pacifist. Would she bear arms for the country? She said no. Would she drive an ambulance? [She said] yes. Then the judge said to him [Aldous], "Do you mean to say that if an enemy were approaching your house that you wouldn't pick up your gun to defend your wife and your home?" He said, "I wouldn't have a gun in my house, so I couldn't."

The judge was very regretful, and said that he would have a special hearing in Washington at Aldous's convenience. [But] they didn't do anything about it. The next trip [to England], they just went on their British passports.

Maria had a navy blue suit and a white blouse. I sent them handkerchiefs with their monograms in red, white, and blue. They sent me a case of champagne splits which I still have, and the card said, "From two very old friends and very new citizens." It was so awful when it didn't work out. I took them home [afterward]. They were coming to my house for lunch, but they wanted to go home. Aldous said that he just wanted to go to bed. He was very much upset about the whole thing.

Don Bachardy (painter, friend)

I first met Aldous and Maria together. It was probably at a party. I saw them at their house, and I remember them coming to a house [Isherwood and I] had in the canyon—that would have been in 1954–1955. We probably met them with Gerald Heard or at the Stravinskys.

Huxley was a very kind, polite man. You know, I used to listen to him talking to other people rather than talk to him myself; and being with Chris [Isherwood] made it easier for me to observe without necessarily having to pull my weight at a dinner party. I was not only young, but I looked actually much younger than my years, and I don't think people expected me to make a big noise at a party, and I didn't. I behaved very discreetly.

[The Huxleys' King's Road home] was a dark house and darkly lit. It's odd to remember that because, of course, with such bad eyesight as he had, it seems remarkable that he wouldn't have wanted it better lit, and I marvel that he was able to get around in it. I remember candles and few, very dim lights. It's funny. I guess that's the house Maria was living in when she died, but Chris said all the houses he knew them to live in here were like that. The one up on Amalfi Drive also was very dark and [had a] peculiarly un-Californian atmosphere. There was always the feeling that there wasn't going to be quite enough to eat. There was something about the food. Maria was a curious hostess in that way. I think probably because she ate like a bird, she never really realized what appetites her guests might have.

We went to the house on King's Road. We had picked up Audrey Hepburn in an apartment she was living in near Westwood and drove her to the Huxleys. I can't remember whether they had met each other briefly or whether this was their first introduction, but I remember Maria especially was keen to meet Hepburn, and Hepburn very anxious to meet the Huxleys—and George Cukor was at dinner. I think it was just the six of us.

Hepburn had put on a very elegant suit and looked very trim and quite something. I don't even think her first movie had been released. I think she had just finished making it. But she'd been in the road company of *Gigi* out here. The Huxleys just might have seen that. I know they were great friends with Anita Loos, and it was an adaptation of hers. I certainly don't think he [Aldous] had a queer bone in his body. In fact, I always thought he was one of those men— there are quite a few of them—who actually find lesbian women attractive or masculine: women who have lesbian tendencies are more attractive to them than just an ordinarily hetero-sexual woman. I have no evidence, just instinct. He was certainly married to Maria, who had great lesbian interests I think.

I always just assumed that may well be the case. They [women] are very much better at being both things at once, at dissembling or keeping their private lives private. They're very good at that. And they often don't see any conflict between their lesbian interests and being married and having a family. The two so easily go together for an awful lot of women.

[Did Aldous ever feel prejudice against homosexuals?] If he had found himself in a totally queer situation at a party with nothing but queer men, I think he might have felt a little bit out of it, but he would have found somebody to talk to. He could always talk to people.

By the early 1950s, Maria and Aldous Huxley (perhaps fueled by his research on spirits for *Devils of Loudun*) began a series of informal experiments in parapsychology, their "Tuesday Evenings." These explorations began with mesmerism, hypnotism, and auto-hypnotism, which Huxley turned to in semi-desperation around the time of his iritis in 1951. Soon, however, these soirées expanded to include mediums, magicians, and soothsayers. There is disagreement about who took these more seriously, Maria or her husband, as the reader will note. Of course, these gatherings only heightened a curiosity Huxley had maintained all his life: in 1937, for example, on his arrival in the United States, one of the first places he stopped was Dr. J. B. Rhine's parapsychology laboratory at Duke University (which is parodied at the opening of the film *Ghost Busters*).

Interest in The Beyond dates back generations in the Huxley family, at least to the Victorian period, when William James and Aldous's grandfather sparred about the existence of ghosts, a lively topic in the scientific circles of the time of the founding of the Society of Psychical Research.[5]

Maria Huxley's physical decline in this period stimulated further parapsychological experiments. Her breast cancer grew more serious, a cancer that probably began in the late 1940s. Maria was dying.

Rose D'Haulleville (sister-in-law)

I would go there sometimes on a Tuesday evening where a whole group of people were invited, and they had different people being hypnotized. It was a party, a hypnotizing party—rather fun. People came after dinner and sat in the living room. There were about fifteen people, and then there was a specialist, Dr. Leslie LeCron. He hypnotized the wife of their dentist [a Dr. Hixon]. A rather small woman, she was sitting on a chair, and she closed her eyes and she started talking about her youth and going through it—the voice had practically turned childish.

Laura Huxley (writer, second wife)

Those Tuesday evenings: experimentally spiritualistic, or hypnotism; they were looking over people who were outstanding in that field, and they would go there for one evening, and that was all. I don't know that those Tuesday evenings lasted very long, not when I was married.

Dr. Milton Ericson was there with hypnosis. There was one man [Leslie LeCron] who I think was a professor at UCLA. When Aldous had iritis, he had gone there. He used very orthodox methods of hypnosis, but he knew what to do, self-hypnosis.

You put yourself under, and then you give yourself an order as though it was from another person, and you say, "Now your left arm is beginning to become very light, and lighter and lighter, it's going to leave the table, and it's going to go up in the air." You actually don't do anything and the arm goes up; that is the first experiment that they teach you. He could do quite a bit of that for practical purposes. When he was alone, when he would want to be in a certain state of mind or go to sleep, or whatever.

On a typical Tuesday evening, there were cold cuts and an assembly of five or six people. There was a medium, I remember. There was [Serge and Jim] Hixon, the dentist and his wife. They are not living in town anymore. They were close friends and involved in hypnosis, too. Everybody would be around the table and somebody would speak. It was all very general. There was one very good medium. I was never in contact with the real medium, Eileen Garrett, with whom they were very friendly.

I remember they had a very heavy round table. It started to go from one room to another. We were in a little living room/dining room, and there was a corridor: the table started to go towards that. It was very funny. There were so many extraordinary things happening all the time. Now that I mention it—yes, it was extraordinary.

Maria was a very good hypnotic subject. One time I noticed that this man was trying to hypnotize me, and he did it in a way that I didn't like—so subtle, I just caught myself in time. He wasn't an ordinary technician.

Ellen Hovde (daughter-in-law)

On Tuesday evenings [beforehand] the Huxleys would go to the World's Biggest Drugstore. It's still there [at the corner of Beverly and La Cienega boulevards in Los Angeles]. It *looked* like the World's Biggest Drugstore: those terrible booths, and lots of loud music, distorted. We sat in booths and ate mixed grills—things that Maria would never allow in the house. It was a huge place, and you could buy records and makeup, and you could eat. You could do all those things. He loved it; he wanted to go to Disneyland. He was always suggesting it, and we never got there. That was for kicks; he did enjoy that a great deal.

A lot of socially radical people today would be amazed at the sort of things Aldous and Maria did. They were very free, in a way that people find it difficult to be nowadays. Maria, goodness knows, was a bisexual. She was not offended by Aldous's interest in other women. She didn't want anything to get hot enough to break them up, but they were interested in exploring what everything was all about. I think by the time I knew them that had cooled out and they were interested in exploring psychic phenomena. We did a great deal of that in Hollywood—that Tuesday group they had!

There was a movie producer, Charlie Barnett. There was

a woman who had little voices in her throat. She could hear their voices even if she was eating or drinking, and she wanted to prospect for gold or she knew where buried treasure was. Then there was someone who could move tables, and then there was a fakir who felt that if everybody stood up and closed their eyes, and he walked behind them—that if you really were in tune with him and trusted him—when you felt the urge to fall backward, you would let yourself go, trusting that he would be behind you and not behind someone else.

[Did anybody fall down?] Oh, yes, I did—no, he caught me. Then we did a lot of hypnosis with [Milton] Ericson, which was fascinating because he was so incredibly good. Maria gave a party, an afternoon party, and everyone knew he was there and he would hypnotize someone. No one knew who it would be, but he would choose someone at the party, and he did. You hardly saw it happen. They went into this routine. It was witty and learned and funny and amazing because it was just so silky the way he did it.

Siggy Wessberg (nephew-in-law)

We stayed at their King's Road place. That's when my aunt Maria died. That place was fun, too, because [on Tuesday evenings] there were always strange things going on. They'd have all these séances and all these mushrooms, and big pots of seeds and God knows what. I'd come the next day and things would sort of be awry, and they'd say, "Oh, we had a little thing last night."

I remember him talking once with my grandmother [Madame Nys, Maria's mother] about people and mixing colors, and he said everybody was going to be tea-colored someday, and there's not going to be really that much problem. Everybody's going to be mixed up. Eventually socialism and capitalism and communism are going to get together, and you won't be able to tell what it is. It's so sad that it's taken so long!

In May 1953, following correspondence with Canadian psychiatrist Humphrey Osmond, then visiting Los Angeles,

Aldous Huxley took mescaline for the first time. At that time the substance was legal, and his experience took place under medical supervision, with a tape recorder there for notes (which he later used in writing *Doors of Perception,* simultaneously one of his most autobiographical and most controversial books).

Several friends from this period are convinced that Huxley unintentionally opened a Pandora's box with his experiments with hallucinogens; certainly his thin volume was widely read on college campuses in the late 1960s amid widespread experimentation with psychedelics. (Dr. Osmond coined the term in a letter to Huxley.) There is no need to restate the drama of that event for Huxley; as his nephew Francis Huxley points out, Huxley had a visual epiphany, stereoscopic vision, which he had sought for years. This "gratuitous grace," as Huxley called it, actually arrived not so much free as the product of fifteen years of spiritual and eye exercises.

In subsequent years, he continued his experiments, and at first proselytized for psychedelics as part of the curriculum of spiritual and ecological education articulated in his novel *Island.* In one sense, these experiments allowed Huxley to assert his scientific impulses that were checked by his childhood blinding.

He was asked frequently how he could justify using an external stimulant to achieve higher consciousness. Huxley gave an illuminating explanation to a niece: "Well, you are very fortunate. [Visualizing] is something which happens to artists, or maybe poets, but you must realize that I have never had any physical contact—eye contact—with anything; for the first time I was seeing those things which I could describe intellectually."[6]

Don Bachardy (friend)

[I remember] *The Doors of Perception*—lots and lots about mescaline; he and Gerald carried on about that endlessly—and LSD.

They were just full of their insights and perceptions, and

of course they were really teasing Chris [Isherwood]. They would go on in detail, and Chris would say, "Well, I want some of this. How do I get some of it?" And they together—whether it was consciously planned or not—made it very difficult for Chris to get any and really withheld it from him. I think it was the jealousy of two older men, who'd led rather tame lives from their point of view, finding this terribly exciting new drug. Because Christopher had had all of his adventures and smoked and drank and lived a very worldly life, they weren't going to make it quite so easy for him to get their drug. So he had to go and get it from some other friend in New York.

Under the influence, Chris said Westminster Abbey looked like the inside of a dead whale. I walked all around London with him one day when he had taken it. Yes, that was a lot of fun.

[I remember] Chris's insight into people's faces. Reds: the color red was absolutely startling to him. That one day in London, I remember, we went to an Italian restaurant with the red and white checkered tablecloths, and he was just dazzled by them. It was overwhelming. We went into the Underground and he had to consciously keep saying, "I mustn't stare, I mustn't let people know that I'm looking at them." But he saw things in people's faces. He felt he could read their lives from their faces.

Oh, he was fascinated. He had a great time, but after he'd taken it two, three, maybe four times at the most, he wasn't interested in going on with it.

I remember thinking at the time that they [Aldous and Gerald] were the complete innocents, in a way, with all sorts of stimulants and drugs—whatever most of us take for granted. They didn't smoke or drink. They had perfectly virginal psyches in that way. This was their first real taste of that kind of chemically induced experience, and yes, I think they were heady with it.

I was very fond of Maria, and Chris adored her. They were very close. She was already sick by the time I knew

her, but she looked wonderful, was full of energy, gave dinner parties, came to parties that we gave. She never complained, never put on a long face.

I remember when I drew Aldous, we took a break and
he showed me an art book. It was a painter he loved, an
Italian. [It was] an art book with quite large reproductions.
He was so excited! He wanted to share them with me. He
asked me if I knew the work. He had the book open and
he had his eyes right down on the reproductions [two inches
away] like that, looking at them and talking while he was
looking, really excited. I think most certainly the mescaline
and LSD gave him a visual experience that he'd never had,
and probably to somebody of his bad eyesight it was extraor-
dinarily exciting.

Gerald was more interested in his spiritual insights that
were influenced by the LSD. I mean he spoke about the
visual experiences too, but I think it was something much
more interior that excited him.

They were very exclusive about it. They would just talk
about it after the event. No, we were never allowed to [join
them]. Yet they gave it to other people. I remember they
gave it to [the photographer] George Hoyningen-Huene. He
came to us and told us all about his experiences, and there
was Chris who had been asking for it for months, and he
knew both of them much better than Huene did.

Betty Wendel (friend)

I was there before and after [he took mescaline for the
first time]. I told you about the folds in his trousers; he had
on blue jeans, but in the book, it says, "in the folds of my
grey flannels." [Later] he said, "Maria wanted me to be
better dressed for my readers."

I asked him about mescaline, and he said that there was
a cane chair with holes in it. He said the holes looked enormous. He said that the crevices in his blue jeans looked like
big gullies and mountain passes.

Peggy Kiskadden (friend)

The World's Biggest Drugstore [where *Doors of Perception* takes place]: I'd taken him there; it was just full of everything, and he just couldn't believe it. (Chemists' shops in England are quite different.) He would wander around and see these really absurd things that you can get. Nostrums, but also all kinds of other things that you can buy in an American drugstore, and he thought they were fascinating. Oh, he was just enchanted.

If you took drugs which released the line between what you really did see and what you wanted to see, [a painter's perspective] would be the first thing that Aldous would see.

He was terribly excited by paintings and knew a great deal about them, and wrote about art. He had a longing to see paintings more clearly, and an extraordinary understanding. He would have been, really, a great writer on art. The other [writings] would have had to take a backseat, if Aldous could have seen.

I think he spent his life wanting to see and needing to see; and with this tremendous interest in painting that he had and the enormous amount of reading he'd done on painting, this was one of the great handicaps that he felt about having a blurred visual perception. So it would seem to be that that would be the natural thing that would bubble right up out of the subconscious.

He was terribly interested in the experience and in the sessions they had. It was a new toy, a new interest, and he was always looking for new interests. He was the sort of person for whom any kind of enlargement of knowledge was of interest.

I can hear him saying, "The World's Biggest Drugstore." His English side would be horrified at making a boast like that, and at the same time fascinated: what in the world is it all about? His curiosity always overcame his distaste for large claims.

I don't think Aldous was aware [of how people would react to his taking mescaline] until great storms of criticism broke. I don't think he was aware of how controversial it would be. When he wrote *The Doors of Perception,* I think he genuinely thought that this was a means of [scientific experiment]. I think he would have been heartbroken to know what this [experiment] led to: the whole drug culture. I'm so glad he died before he had to know the debasing of what, to him, was a scientific experiment.

The whole Huxley slant was always toward discovering something scientifically new, and Aldous, in his way, always picked up his ears when there was something of that sort to be interested in.

Francis Huxley (nephew)

I think my father, Julian, admired Aldous greatly and was slightly envious of his form of intelligence. Aldous, I'm sure, admired Julian's intelligence as well. With, perhaps, a slight question mark over his scientific, humanistic endeavors. He did try to persuade Julian to take mescaline or lysergic acid, but Julian found excuses for not doing so—much to Aldous's regret. He thought it would have been a great opening for my father.

If you read *The Doors of Perception,* or *Heaven and Hell,* you'll understand that suddenly he saw the light in everything. Everything became luminous and colored. The outside world suddenly became pregnant with light. And since he had always been interested in light, when he was in the South of France (he was painting then), his paintings are full of light. He was most interested in light, and in the painters Piero della Francesca, Tintoretto, and Piranesi. He liked the Impressionists a great deal because of light.

He tried to translate what he saw in these terms, but once he took mescaline, suddenly the innate quality of light in his own "light" mind just beamed out, I think. That was what he'd been searching for all his life, after being rather submerged in the sardonic shadows of his cultivated life. He saw the light.

If his eye was taken away from him, that means that a

certain directness was taken away from him. Maybe he was just unhandy in his body; he'd never learned how to use his physicality in the natural way. It'd all gone up to his cerebratonic moments, and he was cut off from his somatic life [in Dr. Sheldon's terms]. I think that was one of the large things that he got in his mescaline experience—the feeling that his somatic life actually provided the light. He had, until that moment, no proper understanding of the relations between the somatic and the intellectual—of the sublimatory moments in life.

He took against Freud in a big way; he couldn't bear to think of the sullyings, the *dirt* that Freud put down upon the spiritual life. That is because his sublimatory mechanism was so geared from an early age that he didn't want to see how it actually worked in himself.

Laura Huxley (writer, second wife)

Aldous and Humphrey Osmond had some kind of an affinity, because Osmond was the most verbal person that you can imagine: very, very fast and extremely bright. Also, they had taken the psychedelic together—which always forms a very important bond. Maria liked him. Maria met him at that session [in *Doors of Perception*]. Then I met Osmond several times, of course.

They were very involved with Osmond because he knew about this orthomolecular psychiatrist (which was not called orthomolecular then; Linus Pauling gave [it] that name later on), referring to using a great amount of certain vitamins for a certain illness.

Aldous got from those experiments exactly what he said on several occasions: there is a basic "all rightness" in the universe in spite of all the agony and the horror. He also wrote [to Humphrey Osmond] that it seems almost obscene to say "God is love," but that's what it is. That's what he found.

Aldous took psychedelic drugs altogether probably ten or twelve times. With Osmond he had taken them three or

four times before we were married, and then I described
two. We had three or four more, maybe five. Then the
last one.

It was never casual. This was very important; it was absolutely one of the most important things that we did. It was
never saying, "Let's have whiskey and soda," or, "Let's have
LSD." [Psychedelics have] been done like that and that is
what brought this horrible abuse—and also this misconception. I think ninety-nine percent of the people think [this
way]. We would plan a psychedelic session very carefully.

There is plenty of research proving that there is absolutely
no difference between a mystical experience through LSD
and the mystical experience through fasting or prayer. You
cannot say [that] the one from mystical experience of a mystic (I don't know which century) differs from the mystical
experience of a person who has taken LSD. Aldous always
said that LSD is an occasion for mystical experience; it's not
the producer—very, very different things.

I don't think he had a mystical experience before he had
the occasion to try mescaline. I did not know him then, you
see. But from his writing you must think that he was on the
verge, or that somehow he knew, or that he just needed the
occasion. It is very difficult to say whether he had those
experiences or whether he simply wanted to have them. He
was sometimes in a state of such delight, much acceptance
of everything, and had such a wide vision of the world without taking [psychedelics]. Once in a while I saw him in that
state; you knew that it was not an ordinary state of mind.
How that was achieved, I don't know: [maybe] it was
through his whole life of study. Suddenly you could see, in
the way that he looked and in the way that he did not speak;
he spoke very little, of course. Once in a while he had that.
It did not happen very often; I remember one or two times.
Sometimes people could feel that he was there, even when
he was not in any special place. People just knew that this
man had something inside that was very high, regardless of
the writing or the pain.

Many of us, we don't have transcendental experiences, so how can we talk about them? There was some kind of emanation from this man that was similar to a transcendental experience. Not often, once in a while.

Probably, after you have taken it [a psychedelic] one time, it's much easier to open up like that. The fear comes; that's why it is bad. That's why some people get in trouble.

[The first trip that we took] was the one that was very important. It was my first [experience] and as a guide he was very extraordinary to ask me: he must have had a certain security in me because he said, "Well, before I give it to you, I take it." You know he wanted to make certain for me that I knew what it was, so he took it and I went there in the morning. It was very good stuff, yes; from Switzerland, from Sandoz. There was research then; it was totally okay to research it.

I wrote [about the second experience] in that book *[This Timeless Moment]* so that I would put down the things that I recalled; because then the memory fades and interpretation comes about. I knew that later on I wouldn't be authentic.

The third trip was with Gerald Heard, a group thing. There were several psychiatrists; I don't remember their names, and I remember a big dog. It was at Gerald's—Mrs. Gage's house [in Santa Monica Canyon] actually. LSD, I think it was. There was a doctor who was giving injections. We left in the middle of the day. By about three or three-thirty, I was already able to drive. Then we came home, and it was a very quiet evening in our home.

What happened? Sometimes it's the same ideas that we have every day, but they have a much greater power. So it's not really always a revelation. Sometimes it's more a confirmation, but by the intensity it almost changes quality; because it's so much more intense. To make a very obvious example, you are always enchanted by a flower; but when you see the same flower under the influence of the substance, you are also enchanted but it is so much more tremendous that it becomes the universal knowledge of a flower.

Naomi Mitchison (friend)

Do you remember his talking about drugs? Well, I was quite interested in this, and I wrote to be a guinea pig to somebody who wanted to try out mescaline. I had a hell of a time! He had said that mescaline [peyote] was being used by some Indians in Canada, and how wicked it was to stop them. I was agreeing about this and saying, "Yes, of course, they should be allowed to take what they wanted." Then I had this terrible experience. When I was in the depths of it, I remembered taking his [Huxley's] book out of the book-case and throwing it out of the window. I wrote back to him saying, "Oh, grow up!" I got all right afterwards.

Jeanne Neveux (sister-in-law)

Aldous talked about [his experiences with psychedelics]: how he did it and why. He thought it was interesting. I think Aldous had little memory of his childhood and things like that. [Psychedelics] brought things back. He had been very upset about his mother's death.

[What did drugs give him?] Curiosity, interest, knowing how it works, what it does, how one is. Of course, nobody knows how drugs helped him to die, because Laura gave him drugs when he was on his deathbed.

Sidney Field (friend)

Alan Watts [author and Zen master] knew Aldous well, and he seemed to think that [bad trips] were definitely one of the effects of LSD. For Aldous, this was just the begin-ning. He had just opened a door, and if other people as thoughtful and as intelligent as Aldous had gone in, it [the public reaction] might have been something else.

I think Huxley never realized that *The Doors of Percep-tion* would take off like [that. He thought] that it would be

1. Portrait of Aldous Huxley by John Collier.

2. Portrait of Maria Huxley by John Collier.

3. Christopher Isherwood, Maria Huxley, and bust of Gerald Heard. (William Caskey, courtesy of Don Bachardy)

4. Huxley residence, Wrightwood California (1946-1949). (Author collection)

5. Huxley residence, Llano, California, 1941-1946. (Author collection)

6. Huxley residence off Sunset Boulevard, Hollywood, California. (Author collection)

7. Trabuco College, Laguna Hills, California. (Author collection)

Nov. 4, 1953
        Investigation in the case of these 2 natz cases (Mr & Mrs Huxley)
is required in order that this Service may present a complete case to the U.S.
Dist Cort in the contemplated DENIAL of both cases because of their unwillingness
to bear arms and their desire to take only that part of the oath "that I will
perform work of national importance under civilian direction etc" WITH ADDED
QUALIFICATIONS OF THEIR OWN as shown by their affidavits attached, taken at the
time of filing their respective petitions. It is also to be noted that they do
not claims any particular religious training and belief, but have only their
personal belief for wanting to avoid bearing of arms and for desiring to take
the above mentioned part of the OATH with their own qualifications.
    Investigations should fully cover Mr Huxleys writings as well as a neighborhood ;
employment and social life of both to determine more fully their qualifications
for citizenship outside of their unwillingness to bear arms.

                                    Barney F. Potpack
                                    Designated Officer

Set for Designated Examiner hearing
11/4/53 R

17   13

8. Declassified documents from U.S. Immigration Service (1953)
    and from the Federal Bureau of Investigation (1943).

Federal Bureau of Investigation

United States Department of Justice
New York, New York

67C

62-7683

                                        April 7, 1943

Director, FBI

            RE: 67C,D

        SPECIAL SERVICE CONTACT
        NATIONAL DEFENSE MATTERS

Dear Sir:

        This is to advise that   was recently requested
to obtain information concerning ALDOUS HUXLEY, subject of an inquiry
in this office,   and als

                    Very truly yours   67C

                    E. E. CONROY
                    Special Agent in Charge

9. The Huxley residence in Hollywood, California (1961-1963).
   (Shirley E. Gerry)

10. Laura and Aldous Huxley on the terrace of their home in Holly-
    wood Hills. (Rose Nys Wessberg)

11. Laura Huxley, about 1988. (Collection of Laura Huxley).

Now More Than Ever

MÜNSTER, 26 — 29 JUNE 1994

LIT

12. Program from the 1994 Aldoux Huxley Symposium in Munster, Germany. (Collection of Bernfried Nugel).

13. Paulette Goddard and Charles Chaplin, 1937. (Academy of Motion Picture Arts and Sciences).

14. Gerald Heard, Christopher Isherwood, Swami Prabhavanda. (William Cuskey, courtesy of Don Bachardy).

15. Aldous Huxley in his writing studio, about 1944, in Llano, California. (Rose Nys Wessberg)

16. D. H. Lawrence and Aldous Huxley, mid 1920s. (Chatto & Windus, London)

17. Juliette and Julian Huxley, 1960. (W. Suchitsky)

18. Francis Huxley, 1990. (Dorothy von Greiff, courtesy of Francis
Huxley).

19. Aldous and Maria Huxley. (Chatto & Windus, London).

just an interesting experiment in the enlargement of consciousness, and that was it.

Aldous said that it increased your sensitivity to the point
where it was like another world. This was the time when
he had discovered LSD and thought this was the most
amazing door to open. Whether he had had an actual experience of this transcendental moment or not, I cannot tell. I
know that he and Krishnamurti [former spiritual leader of
the Theosophical Society] used to debate this. Krishnaji
thought this LSD could take you into a mind-blowing sensation and experience. This could be perfectly legitimate, that
one would experience all kinds of extraordinary openness of
the inner senses—"but this is not what I'm talking about,"
he would say.

Aldous was sort of on the fence. He said, "I have to find
out, taste your liberation and then this to find out if there's
any difference."

More and more as he grew older, he was very much
convinced that there would be a solution to human relation-
ships based on this elimination of the personal self, of the
ego. This, to him, was the thing that impressed him so much
about the LSD, that it seemed to flatten the ego for the
time being.

Krishnaji was always maintaining the intellect was a very
dangerous weapon which had two sharp edges and could
cut against you just as it could cut for you. Aldous would
say, "But it can cut for you in a wonderful way." He would
show you the wonderful things intellect had helped to bring
about, and of course Krishnamurti had to agree.

In 1951, Maria Huxley had a mastectomy; though the cancer had already metastasized into her system, she resolved to
tell virtually no one, certainly not Aldous. Peggy Kiskadden
knew because her husband, Bill, was the Huxleys' medical
adviser. Underlying Huxley's writings and experiments of this
period was probably the semiconscious knowledge that his
two-decade-long relationship with Maria was drawing to a

close. "But what can philosophy do when the soul is utterly broken?" Huxley had written of Maine De Biran at the death of the philosopher's wife. "His unconscious mind pays no attention . . . his body disregards the will's commands." Many feel Huxley was in denial of Maria's illness, particularly during their last summer in Europe, in 1954.

On February 7, 1955, Maria Huxley returned from the hospital to her house to die; Aldous Huxley's account of his death watch, widely quoted, gives a most moving account of her last moments, as he read to her from *The Tibetan Book of the Dead*. As he would write soon afterward, in his now-neglected volume of essays *Tomorrow and Tomorrow and Tomorrow*, ". . . despair is only the penultimate word, never the last. The last word is realism—the acceptance of facts as they present themselves, the facts of nature and of human nature, and the primordial fact of that spirit which transcends them both and yet is in all things . . ."

A year later, he married Laura Archera, a violinist and therapist. Laura Huxley had moved to Los Angeles in the 1940s, working briefly with the Los Angeles Philharmonic Orchestra, then with the film producer Gabriel Pascal as an assistant editor. In the early 1950s, she shared the Huxleys' interest in hypnosis, mesmerism, and parapsychology.

Juliette Huxley (sister-in-law)

Aldous told me that Maria had this operation for cancer, three years before. When she came back from Paris—she'd been in Paris to see a great specialist there, Professor Mondor, the doctor said to her, "Look. It's final. You can't do anything about it. You go back to the treatment you are having in Los Angeles as soon as you can, but I'm afraid it's final."

Then Aldous visited us—he left Maria in Paris and we were sitting in the garden, and I said, "How is Maria?" He said, "Well, she's got little nodules coming out." "Goodness!" I said, "Aldous, that's frightening!" "No, no, it's quite all right. It's normal." He pushed it all out [of mind]. Aldous did not *want* to know that Maria was dying. Maria did not want him to know.

When she died [in 1955], he said he was amputated. He suffered terribly, terribly.

Laura Huxley (writer, second wife)

Ginny Pfeiffer [Laura's longtime companion], Maria, Aldous, and myself went to see Tarquinia and the Etruscan tombs. I think one time Virginia was with us and the other time she wasn't. Maria was glad to go out with me in the car because she said I didn't drink, so she wasn't worried. Sometimes I would meet Aldous in Hollywood, and if Maria wasn't there, I would drive him back. Maria was pleased about that because she knew I wasn't inebriated. I knew that Maria was very, very sick, but not that she was dying because I was never told.

The sickness went very rapidly. She went back and forth from the hospital. I was in Italy at the time. I just assumed that she was in treatment. It seemed that the last time that she came back from the hospital, the doctor told him that it was very bad.

Maria had to do everything. That's when they moved to Melrose, on King's Road, to a big house. (It's not there anymore; they made apartments.) I lived there for three or four months before moving to the [Hollywood] Hills. Yes, she was very tired.

Rosalind Rajagopal (friend)

Once Maria was in the hospital and had an operation. I'd gone down to Hollywood, having had some free time from the [Happy Valley] school or something, and Aldous said, "She's in the hospital; will you get her and take her home?" That was the saddest thing. I went and got her. They lived on King's Road, and I took her home. The house was cold, and he was trying to make a cup of tea for her, and just do everything he could do. Maria was wonderful with him. She just understood everything. When he took the cup of tea to her, it jiggled. He had difficulty with seeing, but he was trying his best to take care of her.

Jeanne Neveux (sister-in-law)

In that last summer, Maria was so sick. We [Aldous and I] went together to a doctor here, a cancer specialist and waited for her. She went to ask him about the cancer she had, and how long she would live. She wanted to know, and she asked him, and he told her. To me, it was awful, but she faced it. She knew, and she wanted to do the things she had to do before she died. In a way, maybe, she did not want to live anymore. She sort of felt that she'd done what she could. She was tired; everything was much too much for her, she couldn't live up to it.

They came to meet us; we were in the South of France, and then they came back to Paris because she was not well.

Aldous didn't want to know. No. He would not know. Well, he paid quite a lot of attention to her, but it was just like that: Aldous, his work, his place in life, his doing. I expect he was very English, in a way. Aren't English people sort of shut in? Maybe they're not like that today, but at one time.

He was very, very good to her when she was ill. But the last time she went into the hospital, she took the car and drove herself to the hospital. Why? Because Aldous couldn't drive. Not because he didn't want to. You see, not being able to do many things does make you live differently.

That summer in 1954, she talked to me a lot about Laura, her friendship with Laura, and who Laura was. Before she was dying, I think Maria arranged things so that it [the marriage] might be.

Aldous got on well with women who liked other women. Who were more attracted by other women. It's a peculiar situation, yes. When people have no preconceived ideas, when they don't think, "this shouldn't be done, that shouldn't be done"—if you're free of all that, then maybe you do some things that other people don't understand.

She [Laura] must have been pretty. She was much younger, she was charming; she was originally Italian. We're all attached to Italy as if we were born there, more maybe. And maybe he was pleased, finally, to protect somebody and help somebody.

Peggy Kiskadden (friend)

Aldous was always fascinated with the thing that was different, and the Loudun experience was, to him, fascinating in a way that it wouldn't be fascinating to me at all. [It was] like many of the extraordinary experiences of the saints that just don't interest me in the slightest. Aldous always had a side that was interested—that's why he would be interested in mescaline, why he would always be fascinated by unusual, by the out-of-the-ordinary. I think that really was the scientist manqué. Aldous always, always, had this curiosity—I always associated it with his loss of sight and the bitterness that he had repressed, and it came out in different ways.

Aldous was very special. You got the impression that this was something that Nature doesn't throw up very often. He was just an extraordinary creature. He had great feelings for others, but maybe he couldn't face that the person he'd depended on from the time he was twenty-two was going to leave.

Maria would rescue him from situations where people were trying to get at him. Anybody as well known as he was always prey to well-meaning people, and Maria would just competently rescue him. She always put him absolutely first. She acted as his bodyguard, but very charmingly, very sweetly. I saw her do it again and again—like a little dachshund coming in and saving a St. Bernard. She'd do it so charmingly that the people wouldn't realize that they'd been just cut out. Aldous would be taken home or whatever. She would say, "Oh, I'm so glad to meet you, too," and then speak for a minute or two, and then say, "I'm sorry, we have to go; we have another engagement." She'd just take him right away. She always did it pleasantly, never crossly.

I think that his disappointment in not being able to study medicine made him very interested in doctors—especially doctors who were a bit off the beaten track. His judgment wasn't very good about who was what Maria used to call a "quack" and who was a legitimate doctor.

I know when they met Laura, Maria thought she was attractive. I suppose Maria would have been capable of suggesting [the marriage] to Aldous, but I think it does stretch one's credulity quite far. After Maria died, I felt that there was a great effort on Aldous's part to be independent, not to batten on anybody else, to show he could go it alone. The silence was killing him; having no one there to talk to must have been very much harder than I thought at the time.

Aldous did his magnetic passes with me when he was up here on Sunday. He had me lie down on the couch, and he would just talk in that lovely voice of his, "You're going to sleep." He did it with his voice, "Now you're going to sleep," that sort of thing, so I don't remember anything specific about it, except I pretended to go to sleep.

Finally, when she knew she was dying, she said, "If Aldous can get on without me, he will," and accepted the fact that she could do no more.

I don't know what he knew [about Maria's cancer]. I don't think he knew enough medicine to know. I know the doctor would have been perfectly frank with him. Whether the doctor would have spelled it out, I doubt. He wouldn't have said, "She's going to die." He would have said, "Unfortunately the tumor was on the inside." You see, Aldous always gave the impression of knowing so much medicine, but when the chips were down, he really didn't.

[I saw Maria in the hospital] looking about as big as a minute—jaundiced. She said, "Aldous says I may come home. Isn't that good of him?" I asked her when she was going, and she thought the next day. That afternoon they brought her home. It was the end of the week that she died. I was with her. It isn't the story that Aldous tells.

Aldous was almost at the end of his tether—Matthew too. I sent them both to sleep and said I'd wake them if she got worse. We had a substitute nurse with her that night who was a snippety woman who kept annoying Maria. I said, "Please leave her alone." She retired to another room and was not there for the rest of the night. I sat beside Maria. Once in a while I would say something—whether she heard it or not, I don't know. Then her breathing was slowing, and so I went and called (this was about 5:00 A.M.) Aldous and Matthew. They came and Aldous talked, because he believed that hearing was the last thing you lost, and that he would be able to give her—and I think it gave him a lot of comfort to talk to her and tell her, "Go, go into the light." If it comforted him, wonderful. Maria was past hearing, I'm sure.

When Aldous saw that she had gone, we sat there for a few minutes. He rose and Matthew and I followed him out. He went into the front room and said, "Oh, it's getting light." I said, "Yes. We must make some breakfast soon." Then we thought who we should notify. We had to notify an undertaker, and we did those painful things that you do. It was clear that he was crying inwardly. You just know when a person's face is stricken.

After Maria died, Aldous assumed a responsibility that Maria had always carried. Maria had always kept in touch and done the writing back and forth. If they telephoned, Aldous would go on the phone, too, but Maria was the guiding spirit. She took care of everything of that sort.

Huxley's place in British letters was secure, and he returned to popular journalism. After a forty-year writing career, with several dozen books published, he was a sought-after magazine writer, judged sufficiently reliable to be trusted with the subject of parapsychology for *Life* and given his own column in *Esquire*.

Following Maria Huxley's death in 1955, Aldous traveled to the East Coast on business and to spend the summer in

Connecticut with his son and his grandchildren, Trev and Tessa Huxley. There Huxley slowly regained his balance and resumed work on a volume of essays on the American West (*Tomorrow and Tomorrow and Tomorrow*, 1956) and his final published novel (*Island*). This was a period of adjustment, ending in his surprise marriage to Laura Archera Huxley and an unsuccessful attempt to mount a dramatic version on Broadway of his novella *The Genius and the Goddess*.

Betty Wendel (friend)

Maria was in the hospital, and I remember so well going there one day, and he was crying. He said, "Maria's being brought home to die." Maria phoned me from the hospital. She said, "I'm going home to die." And I said, "Don't say that, Maria." And she said, "Now let me talk, or I'll be cross. Always see to it that Aldous always has a fresh ribbon on his typewriter."

After Maria's death, he just gradually picked up, and then he went to New York. Rose [Nys, Maria's younger sister] drove him to New York. She was so nervous about taking him. I remember—when they left I took them both a bottle of sherry to take with them. Rose said she was so nervous, and then they started having their sherry together. [How could you tell Aldous was upset?] Because he was very quiet, much more quiet. He used to talk a great deal. I remember sometimes he would ask me to stay when I was going home because he and Maria loved sunsets. They loved the end of the day.

Rose D'Haulleville (sister-in-law)

After Maria died in 1955, Aldous asked me if I would drive him east. That is when I drove east [for New York, left April 20, 1955]. My sister Suzanne said, "You are an ass!" And I said "What do you mean?" "Here," she said, "you travel with Aldous . . ."

They were hoping that I would be the second wife, you see. But it would have been the end of the world; I just couldn't, you know? Because Maria was sitting between us in the front seat, mentally.

We went the long way—via Brownsville, Texas, to see Frieda [Lawrence] and Angie. So, it was very hot. We arrived in Yuma, on the Mexican border—this is on the first day—and we saw there a marriage town. One [chapel] was the Reverend Cockadee's. We were talking and laughing about it.

I wasn't *in* love, but I loved him dearly. I still do. When I try to meditate, or something like that, it's Aldous that comes to my mind more than anything.

Betty Wendel (friend)

In 1955, I was working in L.A. with Aldous [on the dramatic version of *The Genius and the Goddess*], and there was a stage director out here, Arthur Penn, who was working with us. Aldous said, "I'm going away for a few days; I want to take a break and go away for a few days." I didn't know he was getting married. I went home and the phone started ringing. It was reporters from all the newspapers, asking what I knew about it. I said I didn't know anything.

It was all a great mystery to me. He wasn't secretive at all. Maybe he didn't tell you anything he didn't want you to know, but you didn't get a sense that he was secretive. He would confide about some things—but never about Laura. After Maria died, he talked about Maria a great deal, he cried so much after she died and was so miserable. When Matthew was here, Matthew and I took walks and talked about it. Then he and Aldous went away for a week. We were working at the time, and I thought Aldous might not want to work anymore. Then he phoned one day and said, "Can you come here tomorrow?" He was crying. I had never seen him cry at any other time.

Ellen Hovde (daughter-in-law)

He took LSD after Maria died, some time after. We were together, and he said, "You know, it was the first time I could really cry." He cried and cried about that, but it wasn't his way to show a lot of feeling openly.

We were talking before about LSD and mescaline and its effect on him, and I think it did show him in the old Zen way of a kick-in-the-ass or a blow-on-the-head; the thing, nonverbally, which he didn't know before. He couldn't even remember his mother who died when he was [fourteen, November 29, 1908]. He had no memory of her at all. He could block those things out.

If you've ever taken LSD, you know it usually hits you where you're most blocked, and it hit him hard. He was very grateful.

Aldous always worked in the morning. We'd have breakfast together, and he would invariably—I don't think he ever changed his routine—go into his study and work until lunch. I think the summer was chiefly memorable for being so incredibly hot. There wasn't a breath of air stirring that entire time. I made Aldous a pair of pedal pushers out of an old pair of pants, and he looked like a stork because his legs were sticking out.

After lunch we would go off, and we would drive wherever or do whatever we thought of. We drove a lot, and we walked on the beach. He was a great sand artist. He would work again from five to seven and then we'd eat dinner. Then I would read to him until almost midnight.

Aldous had that side to him—get in there and do a little something for fun. I remember when Tess [his granddaughter] was about three he came to visit us in Connecticut. We had a rabbit in a wire cage. I still remember him walking off with Tess on the end of his finger. They were going to pull the feet of the rabbit out from underneath [the cage], which they could do because the bottom of the cage was wire. The rabbit would squeak, and they both loved it! [laughs]

Laura's fascinating. She's European, she is very musical; her interests dovetailed into his and Maria's. I think he felt romantic about her, cared for her a great deal. She was in many ways the opposite of Maria. Her attitude was "Hey, you're a grown-up; you don't need to be taken care of—I need to be taken care of." That was a novelty! I know a lot of his friends were very, very upset because they felt that she was neglecting him and leaving him on his own to struggle and this and that. I think there was a certain amount of that, but on the other hand, I think it was very freeing for him, too, because he was expected to cope. And he did.

I was a little surprised that he didn't get in touch with us [before his second wedding], especially with Matthew. But I don't think that it honestly occurred to him that Matthew would be mortally wounded. I think that if someone had done that to him, he wouldn't have been mortally wounded. So he couldn't understand why anyone else would be mortally wounded.

Francis Huxley (nephew)

I remember him in 1955, at the conference run by Eileen Garrett in the South of France. This was a very nice rest hall run by her man-friend Jean. I was sitting at a table three tables away; the place was very crowded. Suddenly, over the hubbub, I heard Aldous's voice—like a cello—sing over everything; one could hear every intonation of his voice. He was so resonantly pure in his own voice that he could be heard over the hubbub. He just put his voice into it, and his voice sang his meaning—or "cello'd" his meaning—very beautifully.

When Aldous began to speak, they would sit back and enjoy it. It usually was a well-formed piece that he had to say—with some fascinating and phenomenal phrases that would come out from time to time.

I think Aldous liked Laura because she had a darting, kingfisher mind. She would talk, and then a little ripple upon the conversational stream would attract her. She'd plunge into it and come up with a minnow and swallow it, go and perch on a bough and "kingfish" to herself and then off she'd go.

I think Aldous was very pleased with his life in this surrounding. She kept him well stocked with small talk. He didn't have small talk, as far as I could see, but I'm told that he always liked gossip very much. He liked the company of pretty and beautiful women, and he liked the company also of large minds with obsessions.

In 1956, he and Laura invited me out to supper. I had just had my first book on the Brazilian Indians, *Affable Savages*, published and Laura provoked me to say, "So what are they like?" So I started telling stories about these Indians. I dredged up the more grotesque and remarkable anecdotes that I could think of. Laura was delighted. Aldous kept on eating his lunch, and he never said anything. I went away feeling that I had fallen into the adolescent forms of mania and had vastly disappointed my dear uncle Aldous, whom I really had wished to impress. I went away very cross with myself.

Two or three days later I went to see Eileen Garrett, who told me that Aldous had been around telling all my stories and roaring with laughter as he told them. Then I began to understand Aldous.

Laura Huxley (writer, second wife)
Maria took much more care of Aldous than I did. Maria married Aldous when they were both very young. I already had a life, and I had my interests and my ambition and my careers and projects all the time, so it [our marriage] was totally different from that point of view. Aldous seemed to enjoy it, though. Every time that I had a new project [such as her book *You Are Not The Target*], he was delighted no matter what it was.

Juliette Huxley (sister-in-law)
I think they made a pact that Laura would go on with her career, and Aldous accepted it. There are legends that Maria chose Laura. I don't believe that, but it's possible. Maria was very conscious that Aldous should not be left alone to look after himself.

Eileen Garrett was a genuine medium; she really had a gift. When Maria died, she claimed to have talked to Maria. Aldous told it [the story] to me in New York when we met at a party about six months after Maria died. I was walking back with him to his hotel, and he said, "Eileen has been in touch with Maria. Maria said to her, "I was helped when I died by Aldous talking to me about Mister Ekot and the Tody—the book of the Tody." Eileen Garrett said to Aldous, "I don't understand Ekot. I never heard of anybody called Ekot, nor Tody. Tody means nothing to me. I think something has got completely wrong."

Aldous knew Mr. Ekot was Meister Eckhart, and Tody was the [Bardo Thödol] *Tibetan Book of the Dead*. "Well," I said, "Aldous, what can we believe?" He said, "I don't know. I cannot know." And he went into his hotel and shut the door.

Aldous had a great hunger for that fringe of unknowing. He was always reading books about it. Maria was also deeply interested, Laura less so. You might say he had an inward eye which revealed some things. One doesn't know the limits of human apprehension—human sensitivity.

He talked about his experimentation with hallucinogens, and he offered Julian LSD. Julian said no. You see, Julian had had several nervous breakdowns, and he didn't feel that his nervous constitution was really suitable for experiments which took him so far out of his experience. He was afraid of risking it.

Betty Wendel (friend)

[Work on the play of *The Genius and the Goddess* had moved to the East Coast.]

We adapted the play—the book, really, and stuck to that. I would write a certain section, and he'd go over it and change some of the dialogue. We'd meet every couple of days and talk about it.

Aldous and I worked separately, and then we would meet. He'd go over mine, and I'd go over his. But because of his eyesight, he didn't visualize anything. He'd say, "Any entrances and exits you'll have to write." It was the strangest thing. I remember once he said that somebody went up the stairs and then came in from the garden.

We were both in the same hotel, and I went down to see the manager. She said, "Have you seen Mr. Huxley?" I said, "No." She said, "Well, I wish you'd go up on the roof because I'm worried to death about him; he's acting in such a peculiar way." There was a sudden hot spell, and he'd bought one of those drip-dry suits, and it said on it to wash and let dry. He was going around and around on the roof. I said, "What are you doing?" He said, "Trying to get this damn suit dry."

Once I had stayed up all night writing some things and trying to keep as much of Aldous's writing as possible [in the script], and then he wrote me and said that you couldn't write scenes with Scotch tape. That was exactly what he had been doing all the time, so I was sort of annoyed about that. It was precisely what he did.

The producers did some sneaky things. The director once arranged an interview with Aldous. My husband was there, and he said, "Why don't you and Sandy go out to dinner?" He suggested some faraway restaurant. When I came back, there was a note in my box at the hotel to come right to the theatre. I did, and they were rehearsing some scenes the director had written that were terrible.

That's when [Laura and Aldous] left. I wanted to leave, but I couldn't. The play was a great success in Oxford, with Constance Cummings, and there were glowing reviews. They toured very successfully for about six weeks, and then it came into London.

After he left Philadelphia, I wrote some things [for the dramatic adaptation of *Genius and the Goddess*]. The people in the company read them to him on the telephone, and he said that he didn't like them. Then he later apologized and said he had said that because he wanted to go back to Philadelphia, and Laura wouldn't let him.

We were all treated poorly. Alan Webb, who played the Genius, saved my life. I was with him all the time.

Aldous was terribly anxious to get it on. He just wanted to because he had a couple of failures, and I don't even know what they were. He very much wanted a successful play. The producer wrote us that he wanted to put in a long speech that he had written. We cabled him not to, and he did anyhow. That was why the play failed, I think.

The characters in *The Genius and the Goddess* are supposed to represent the Curies [Marie].[7]

Don Bachardy (friend)

I remember hearing about this [the 1957 production of *Genius and the Goddess*] production in New York. I think it closed almost immediately.

I don't think he [Aldous] was a bitter man. I never felt any kind of bitterness or regret, and he never complained. He was so lively. You caught it right away; he was so interested in what he was talking about that it became exciting.

Chapter V
Hollywood Hills (1956–1963)

In the last half-dozen years of his life, Aldous Huxley, a man who twenty-five years before could barely be persuaded to speak from a podium for any reason, became a public and university lecturer. His income no longer came primarily from his books—although *Brave New World* had entered American high schools in paperback form—but from visiting lectureships at the University of California, Berkeley, The Center for the Study of Democratic Institutions (Santa Barbara), M.I.T., and the Menninger Clinic in Kansas. He supplemented this with commissioned essays for the Long Island newspaper *Newsday* (which were later published as *Brave New World Revisited*) and by essays for mass-circulation magazines: *Esquire, Life, The Atlantic*—works with a scientific or didactic intent quite different from his journalistic pieces commissioned by *Vogue* and *Vanity Fair* in the 1920s and '30s. These essays (and several prefaces) catalog his concerns in the 1950s: parapsychology, human ecology, overpopulation, and the meaning of Indian religions in contemporary life. It was a period not so much of new beginnings as of continuing concerns, particularly about education and the visionary impulse. Huxley's stint at M.I.T. coincided with the famous experiments at Harvard on the psychology of con-

119

sciousness under Timothy Leary and Richard Alpert—the beginning of a psychedelic movement about which Huxley had reservations. Similarly, in 1961 Huxley taught at Berkeley as the disarmament and civil-rights movements swelled.

Ellen Hovde (daughter-in-law)

Aldous really always looked the same to me. I never thought that he changed much. He got a bit grayer, but he was always extremely thin and somewhat stooped, and he had that kind of walk that people have when they don't see terribly well—they put their feet down very carefully.

He had a beautiful head. My goodness, what a wonderful head he had, very thin, fine-boned, a beautiful face. And he threw his head back when he talked and laughed. He had a sporty sense of humor.

I think that he was much more a person of the New World than the Old, although he wouldn't have said so. He also was, of course, incredibly European.

For some who are that smart and that learned and so different from most people, they live in a very different world themselves. They can be very fond of other people, but they're sort of like a pet cat or something. Not all the time, but there's a certain amount of time when you must feel like you live in a fine land and all these people don't quite speak your language. And you certainly don't speak theirs. The references that you bring to a subject are so different. I mean, Jesus, how are you going to talk to people? It's with a kind of grace that people like that live in the world.

As a person he was more and more at peace the longer I knew him. I don't think he'd found nirvana but I think he felt more relaxed in the world for some reason. I don't know exactly why. I don't even know whether it was that we all were more relaxed around him. I felt that we could push him around, and kid him, and hug him, and not take him so seriously. Both ways that was true. He would enjoy being, as he said, a "living monument" occasionally, and he'd go on these tours to Brasília, crazy places. But, in fact, I think he was very grateful to have a domestic life, an ordinary life, because the other life went on relentlessly in his mind.

I think as he got older, he's one of the few people who got more open and more available rather than closing down and becoming more set in his ways. I think by the time he died, he was very young.

Jacob Zeitlin (bookseller and literary agent)

After Maria's death, I saw relatively little of Huxley except when he would get away, and I saw nothing of Laura. He used to come to the shop sometimes, by himself, and he would wander around La Cienega Boulevard. God, you'd see him crossing the street, and you'd be sure that somebody would hit him because he wasn't aware of whether there was a green light or not. I remember one day I came in, and he was in the back room. He and one of my children were playing string figures, and he was very good at it.

There were several things in which I was not in sympathy with him. First of all, I thought *Island* was an inferior book. A great deal of it was written to please Laura and Ms. Pfeiffer [Mrs. Huxley's close friend]. The other thing was his involvement with mescaline. I never approved of that. I felt that, first of all, it was inconsistent with the very idea of mysticism that he admired; they didn't need the artificial aids to achieve their mystical states. I told him I felt this was the wrong path. I also felt that it gave sanctions to all the people who wanted to indulge in psychedelics and that it would make respectable what I felt should not be respectable. He gave it the sanctions of his own endorsement.

Laura Huxley (writer, second wife)

I have had problems because of the drug connection, because of ignorance. People speak about "Drugs," you know.

I don't pronounce my "r" really clearly, so sometimes I

found that everybody was quite nice and not upset. They thought all the time that I was speaking about "Dogs" not about "Drugs." So I was not attacked so violently as I could have been. "Can she do all that with dogs? She must be pretty good."

When we married, we moved in together. Life had really taken a totally different turn. The difference was mainly that I was not as giving as Maria. I was interested in myself, where I think she was interested mainly in him. I already had a career. I was thinking of many things that I wanted to do, so that I did not give him all this time that Maria did. She really lived through him, from what I understand.

He knew very well from the beginning that I was . . . that I would be a different kind of companion than Maria was. Can you imagine, over thirty years they were married.

Actually the difference amused him, I think. He really never knew what was going to happen next with me. He sort of liked it. Aldous never had a secretary, and he never wanted one. First of all there was a new input of communications now. He couldn't take it. He couldn't do it all by himself, although he was very quick and very organized, there was so much more now. If he would be alive now, it would take fifty times as much paper.

He would write a few letters, very quickly. It would take him ten minutes to write a letter at the most, a beautiful letter. With a few telephone calls, but he would do most by letter, because then it was done, finished.

[Was Aldous depressed?] Once he had taken some antibiotics, and the antibiotic robbed all the B vitamins which are connected in a fashion. So that time we started right away with a strong few days of B vitamins. Sometimes he would get a little bit [depressed] if he had a problem in writing. But whenever these things happened they were very short; soon he would say, "Oh, it's just one of those silly things of being so involved with my own little problems." He would throw it away and say, "How silly." And they [the periods of depression] were always short.

Aldous was in very good health in those years: '57, '58, '59. People noticed and mentioned it to me. He had a general well-being, I think.

When he would go away, and he was away alone (which everybody was surprised about), he would cook all kinds of vegetables for breakfast, a very good idea. In the house he did very little cooking. When he was alone, he managed for himself perfectly well. One time he said, "I'm going to write a little book about soups." Sometimes in the morning we would make a soup out of dried beets and dried green vegetables in powder. The colors were so beautiful. If you put a drop of oil on top, it's golden on top of this red and green, and we were fascinated. We had sherry often before dinner, in the beginning when we were married. We had wine sometimes, half a glass.

He would take care of me anytime, but he would leave me a lot of space around; he was never overpowering. He would [offer love] a little bit, without forcing. But if I would speak about going on a fast, he would say, "A fast is very good for those people who are forty pounds overweight, but you—after all, what are you, 110?"

Typically, the weather [in Hollywood Hills on Deronda Drive, where the pair moved after marriage] was very clear. He would awaken always about eight-thirty and go in his studio and write—usually he was writing, and sometimes he was also reading, naturally. Sunday he always wrote letters. He had no secretary. He did everything himself, very quickly. Then we would have lunch. Sometimes I was there, sometimes I wasn't. In the afternoon, if there were some people to be seen, we would see them about four or five o'clock.

He made his own tea if I wasn't there. If there was somebody visiting, we would serve tea. In the evenings we usually stayed home, but if there was a concert or the theatre we went out to dinner with some friends. Usually we invited people on Saturdays because then we had the help of this wonderful person, Marie LePut, and she would come and cook so I didn't have to worry about the cuisine. For lunch on Saturday, we never had more than eight people altogether, but always one or two. Once in a while we went to the Stravinskys' in the evening. Then Stravinsky also came for lunch.

Aldous traveled alone most of the time. I didn't travel with him. I would go to the airport with him, yes. One evening, though, I was out. He took a walk in the dark, and he didn't see there was a hole and he fell. That was the only time that something happened because of his sight, and he was a little bruised.

Juliette Huxley (sister-in-law)

I don't think Aldous ever had mortal fear about himself. He accepted what came—except perhaps, his death. That was a nightmare.

The date Huxley began *Island* is not known precisely— probably in the early 1950s: "Aldous had a lot invested in *Island;* this was what *Brave New World* should have been and wasn't," Matthew Huxley reflected. Huxley often pointed out how much more difficult it was to write a utopia than a dystopia, as he struggled to balance narration and exposition. Dedicated to Laura, the novel was so full of digressions that his editors took the unprecedented step of asking for deletions.[1] Much of the spiritual education Huxley describes therein is drawn from the spiritual leader Krishnamurti, to whom Huxley drew closer in his remaining years.

For an alternate representation of the views in *Island,* one might explore the published lectures Huxley gave in Santa Barbara in 1959 (*The Human Situation,* Harper & Row, 1978), which he repeated at M.I.T. in 1961. His themes in these lectures included human ecology, overpopulation, and the relationship between nationalism and war—the very issues discussed in fictional form in his last novel. In comparing these with the exposition of *Island,* a careful reader might find not only that Huxley's lecture style had become epic in scope but that this struggle to finish the novel stems from his continuing battle between expressing ideas in fictional, versus essayistic form.

Laura Huxley (writer, second wife)

He had some difficulties in doing the skeleton, or structure, of *Island.* He never had any problem in writing essays or prefaces. That was very easy. He would enjoy it. Then he had that period in New York [1956–1957, during the pre-production of *The Genius and the Goddess*] where he was really treated so badly. It was terrible.

As far as his writing problems—after a day or two or three he would say, "Nothing—I am stuck—and then I get these stupid ideas that I cannot do ever anything again." He would just kick it around.

He would admire a novelist like D. H. Lawrence, and he said that he was not that kind, that it was harder for him. Once in a while he would say something about losing his own powers of fiction and then laugh about it. So it [the writer's block] was not important.

He didn't lose his interest in pacifism. He wrote a great deal about it. I gave you that piece of that talk he gave in '63—that was the last year of his life. *Science, Liberty and Peace* [1946] was already there, and the [pacifism] continued all the time. We went to Sicily to see Dolche—this kind of Italian Gandhi—and Aldous wrote a preface for his book because, in Sicily, the situation was terrible. That was in 1959, and he was always in touch with things like that.

One time he said, "Why does one take so much time looking at television?" I said, "How do you get the news?" (He had this small little radio.) "In just fifteen minutes in the morning, I get all the news, and sometimes in the evening." He wanted to know why I watched, like a researcher looks at it.

Abigail Bok (friend)

The first recollections I have [of Aldous Huxley] are of going over to his house, being taken over by my grandmother [Peggy Kiskadden]. Aldous had a big bandage or brace around his neck, and I was introduced. Then my brother and I were sent off to play with [Virginia Pfeiffer's] young adopted children. I just remember him sitting in a chair or out on the terrace. He was very quiet. I think he did speak, but not much. He appeared to have some pain associated with speaking.

My grandmother felt that [taking drugs] was a fallacy. It was something that some people might do in the privacy of their own homes as a scientific or as a spiritual, philosophical experiment, but she didn't think it would help and she didn't think it had helped Huxley. She didn't think anybody else should try to help themselves in this way. I don't know that I agree with her.

Dorris Halsey (agent)

Island is, of course, a work that is nearest and dearest to Laura's heart because it was the one book that was written during her tenure. He made very important and very beautiful statements in that, but [in fact] the book came out of a time of turmoil in the 1960s.

Aldous's books are difficult to transpose into film. *Brave New World* was acquired by RKO and was finally made by NBC as a miniseries. Now they're trying to make a musical out of it. That's one area in which I am involved. I have a musical Broadway contract for *Brave New World;* I have one for *Island.* I had talked about *The Genius and the Goddess* also, for a remake as a motion picture.

Aldous was the forerunner of the commercial jingle—this is how his characters spoke in *Brave New World.*

In May 1961, sparks, then flames, blew up the Hollywood canyons to the house of Laura and Aldous Huxley (who was at that moment finishing the manuscript of *Island*). Within

hours, all his possessions had burned: his library, his manuscripts (and those of D. H. Lawrence and others), his correspondence—much like the potlatch of possessions a monk
undergoes before taking his vows.

Accounts of this ordeal vary dramatically. Recollections of
Huxley's response offer a case study of the diversity of oral
evidence. Some say he was relieved; others, devastated. His
published letters suggested a philosophical resignation.

Peggy Kiskadden (friend)

It came over the radio. We knew there was a fire all the
way along. Then we were in touch and found out they'd
gone down to this little hotel, and so I got a lot of my
clothes together and took them over to Laura, thinking that
she'd lost all her clothes. I understand she saved her clothes,
but did not save the little trunk that had all the letters,
when they [Maria and Aldous] were separated—when Maria
was seventeen and Aldous was twenty-two. That was right
there in the garage, the little trunk was up on a shelf, and
it should have been saved. It had gone everywhere with
them, always, wherever they went.

She said, "We've lost everything." So of course, I threw
together underwear, clothes, shoes, and so on, and took
them to her.

Aldous was completely self-controlled about it. He took
the Englishman's view of distancing himself from the disaster and being slightly humorous about it. It took all his
books for one thing, which were extremely important.

He said humorously, "It was very interesting to start life
with only what one stood up in." He never would have
betrayed any grief about it, though I'm sure he felt great
grief over losing his books, which were annotated and so
on. He said, "It's rather like beginning with no past. It's
like being born again." He just was amused about it, and
then he went on and stayed with Gerald.

Aldous didn't like to talk much about the fire. It was
something that happened, and that was that. From the time

Maria died, Aldous ceased to have the same interest in living, and if the house burned, well, the house burned.

Laura Huxley (writer, second wife)

[After the fire] somehow I didn't touch anything, although [we were] in Ginny [Pfeiffer]'s house. I should have taken some things that I knew were irreplaceable and also even money—there was some stock—but I didn't do it. Aldous was at home. I had just come down the hill to drive someone to the market.

No, it was very strange, because usually in emergencies I am quite prompt; instead, I was passive. Aldous remembered more things. He took his manuscript and a few clothes and down we went. I got so mad—he disappeared all of a sudden. He had gone and taken a ride with some boys to see something. He went for a ride! All of a sudden he wasn't there, and when he came back I was really upset. And he said, "Well I just went with some guys in the car."

I picked up my violin and a few clothes, I think. And I picked up a very nice pin. Maria's letters were upstairs in the attic, but his letters to her were right there. I could've picked them up.

He only brought out the manuscript of *Island*. We had a lot of manuscripts—D. H. Lawrence's and others—in a studio. It was all covered with this library of thirty years.

Fire is hypnotic, I think. There I was, on the top of the hill, and the windows were open and I saw the curtains going towards the fire. The curtains were very light and went through the windows. There was something delightful—the room that I am thinking about was white and the flame outside just gave the right reflection on the walls and the flowers. The flowers weren't arranged very well [normally], but that day the flowers were perfectly arranged. And the light—I cannot give you any rational explanation.

Afterwards we stayed in the hotel for a while, and then he went to Gerald for two weeks, or one week. In the meantime, Ginny had bought a house, and we were trying to move in and get it organized. After [that], Aldous went to Europe, and I followed him after two weeks. I met him in Geneva.

He was invited everywhere, but I think that there was a room [with Gerald], while he was finishing *Island,* and Gerald was there. It was a very short period actually. I don't think that we really moved into this house until we came back [from Europe].

At first I think he was really taken aback, because of all the papers. But it didn't last long. He used to quote Ignatius of Loyola, when they asked him, "What would you feel if this tremendous organization, the soldiers of Christ, the Jesuits, would be destroyed?," and he said, "Well, ten minutes of meditation and it would all be finished."

We had a lovely time in Europe that summer, very lovely. He was still finishing *Island.*

Lawrence Powell (librarian)

I spoke with him after the fire. "Well, I guess the Lord wanted to emphasize that I can't take it with me." He took it in an amused [fashion]. Didn't brood on it.

Jacob Zeitlin (bookseller and literary agent)

After the fire, I don't think he was at peace. I think it was very hard for him to remain philosophical. He said to me, "It's easy to talk about separating yourself from material things, but there are some material things it's very hard to separate yourself from. In my case you're talking to a man without a past, because my notebooks were destroyed." His diaries were very important to him. He depended on them greatly for jogging his memory and for remembering certain things that took place. I think a great deal of his writing grew out of these diaries.

I think he was greatly depressed after the fire. He just felt like he'd lost some very important links with life. Well, you know, by that time, he knew he had this cancer [of the tongue], and he had radium needle treatments. He was under no illusion.

Aldous called me after the fire. He was living at Christopher Wood's house [where Gerald Heard was living]. He asked me to come out. So we made an engagement, and I went out one evening. He said that he had a list of some of the things that had been destroyed, and he wanted to make an insurance claim, would I put an evaluation on them? He gave me that list. I said, "Where is Laura?" "Oh," he said. "She's living somewhere else."

He talked about his diaries, and he said, "You know, I'm a man without a past, because the whole source of my writing was my diaries, and with them gone I don't see how I can ever write any more."

Doris Halsey (agent)

Huxley's reaction to the fire was more stoic than anything I can imagine. That was an incredible loss, it was a blow.

Ellen Hovde (daughter-in-law)

The fire was horrifying, but I remember writing to him that he must feel incredibly light, and he wrote back saying, yes, he did, that if you lose everything, the weight you've been carrying is gone. I thought that if I lost everything, that's how I would feel. I think he did feel that and then, what happened, of course, what would happen to anyone, is you start reaching for something and it isn't there. The thing that we all felt so bad about was Maria's letters—there was a trunk that had all the photos and all the letters and all the journals.

He was going to write an autobiography and he couldn't. I remember having lunch with him at the Plaza Hotel one time, and I said, "Why don't you write one?" And he said, "But I've lost everything. I have no records. I have nothing."

Laura Huxley (writer, second wife)

When [after the fire] we moved into this house [Virginia Pfeiffer's], we had dinner together in the evening. We did a great deal of talking. He had his room up here, and break-fast together with the children and Virginia, and dinners. I was in my studio many of the days, not every day.

We all came to live here [on Mulholland Drive, Holly-wood], which happens to be the best house around, or one of the best. Then he was a famous man, which he didn't pay attention to; neighbors were usually reserved, and Vir-ginia was very, very busy. After a fire there are all these things you have to do. I was very busy, and I was writing all the time. Aldous was writing *Island,* so we did not do the customary invitation to the neighbors ("We are newcomers here"), which I think they took as being too snobbish.

When they wanted to knight Aldous, I thought that would be such a burden: for me and for him, too. As soon as I mentioned it he said, "Oh, I'd better write a letter." He wrote this letter that I've been trying to find. You know we were living here, going around in shorts and so on, and carrying out the garbage.

Siggy Wessberg (nephew)
Once we were at the last home he had, with Laura. I guess it was pretty close before he died because he had moved from the house where the fire was. There was a kid across the street who would get out and wax his red Alfa Romeo every Sunday, and Aldous just thought it was funny. He thought if he waxed this car anymore, there's not going to be any paint. That kind of culture, he couldn't grasp it.

Laura Huxley (writer, second wife)
[Regarding his death], I don't think that he would think in terms of omens. Some people might be very surprised at my interpretation. (There is always a difference about interpreta-tions, which are thought of as objective.) After the fire, he was getting more sick, naturally, because he already had cancer.

Even before the fire, Aldous Huxley had intimations of mortality, to paraphrase Wordsworth. A casual bump on his tongue was apparently misdiagnosed, leading to a spreading cancer of the tongue. Faced with the choice between a tempering cure (radium needles) and surgery (which would have impaired his speech), Huxley chose the former. Soon the cancer returned and metastasized. The sixty-nine-year-old died on November 22, 1963—his passing largely unnoticed by a world mourning the assassination that day of John F. Kennedy.

Many questions persist about his last years: did he reach that unitary knowledge, that enlightenment that so obsessed him?[2] Peggy Kiskadden thinks not; Matthew Huxley believes he did—only to lose it and endure "a long dark night of the soul" and he tried fruitlessly to recapture the moment.

In the preface to *Look Homeward, Angel,* Thomas Wolfe asks, "A leaf, a stone, and unfound door—which one of us has known his brother?" One might conclude that Huxley knew his brother and sisters too well; which is why he introduced serpents into his final Eden, in *Island.* Like the hero of that novel, the cynical journalist Will Farnaby, in the end Huxley prepared himself for that roomful of light, to which he and other Buddhists aspire, "the dear light that, like everyone else, he had always preferred to his torture."[3]

In his Hollywood novel, *The Last Tycoon,* F. Scott Fitzgerald writes that there are no second acts in American lives. Yet, in his American years, Aldous Huxley had a new beginning. He had journeyed from *Eyeless in Gaza* to *Island* (Eyeland), the country where even the blind have visions. According to Laura Huxley, he died at peace.[4] To Christopher Isherwood, he was like a galleon, sinking quietly into the deep.[5]

Peggy Kiskadden (friend)

I don't think Aldous had a mystical experience; I think he wistfully hoped for a mystical experience. I think that this interest, which Gerald Heard had a great deal to do with fostering, was always latent in Aldous. The bitterness and shock humor of the early books was the frustration of [his blindness].

When Aldous had something on his tongue, he went to the dentist and the dentist scraped it—thereby spreading the cancer. It was a wicked thing. He'd gone to the Menninger Clinic to deliver some lectures, and he went to a dentist there. The dentist did that. Aldous came back and didn't mention it to us at all. Then, of course, the thing began to grow. Bill [Kiskadden] was then appealed to and he said, "I think you've got to go into the Good Samaritan and have some specialists look at this." They said, "You, see, this has spread, Mr. Huxley, and the only thing we can do is to cut [it] out. It's on your vocal cords—quite a bit. We'll have to operate because there's no way we can kill it where it is. He and Laura said, "Well, that's mutilation. We have to think." They decided between them to leave the hospital without being discharged, and they just skittered away. I said, "Bill, what do we do?" He said, "We don't do anything. He is a great big man. He has got to face up to what he has done." In the end, Aldous went to another doctor up North.

Well, of course, it was the proliferation of the original cancer—all of it, and by that time his voice was gone and he could only whisper. There was nothing else to be done. All you could do was love him.

It's very odd that a man who had such an enormous intellect could be so naive about matters of health. It may go way back to his mother dying and then his brother dying— both events were very traumatic to him. Maybe deep down in him, he felt that conventional medicine let them die.

Laura Huxley (writer, second wife)

We knew he had cancer. The doctor that we went to then, whom Aldous liked very much, gave both of us less grave news than it really was. We really didn't think that it was very bad in the beginning. First there was a great shock, because [the cancer] was in the tongue; then he did not have the operation. [He] had the [radium] needles and felt very well. The prognosis was very good, so that it was not one of those things that would worry us all the time.

Then he had the second gland off, and that wasn't so good. It was horrible. The person undergoing the biopsy is weak and still under an anesthetic, the doctor marches in and tells him, "Well, you have cancer of the tongue so we are going to make a sketch."

Besides, this surgeon wasn't his regular doctor. It was just somebody who came; his hands were trembling. "We are just going to cut off half of your tongue, and then you take some therapy . . ." And I listened to all this, and I said, "Out. Out we go. Let's get dressed."

Aldous got dressed and had his luggage, and they called, "Where are you going with the patient?! Send him in!" And before they could recover, we were out. I had my car downstairs. And then I said, "We won't pay any attention to that man. He's a butcher and that is not the way to treat this." I remembered seeing this Dr. Cutler once, and I said to Aldous, "Let's see what we are going to do." Because there are so many ways [to treat cancer], and I had quite a bit of experience with it.

This was all very strange. I said, "Remember Dr. Cutler?" He said, "I remember. I know who he is. Dr. Cutler." We called up and within an hour after we left the hospital we were at Dr. Cutler's office. He said, "Don't worry." He gave very encouraging words, and said, "There is nothing to cut off." He used instead needles, small [radium] needles. (Later on, while I was in London, Aldous found that two different schools competed with each other at the expense of the patient: one school wanted to cut off as much as possible and the other wanted to treat without this drastic approach, which is current now.)

Anyway, things went quite well. He had one week [in the hospital] after the needles; that was regular. Then he came home because we had an engagement to give a seminar just over the border in Mexico, in Rancho de Puerta. It was the first time that I even witnessed a seminar, and he was the main person. It was a very interesting seminar, the first of its kind.

He wasn't feeling well, and in fact he did not come to the seminar. That was very upsetting because I was down there every day. First I went, and we thought maybe he would come in two or three days. Ginny Pfeiffer was taking care of him then, and he wasn't getting strong enough. So that was difficult. Finally, I, knowing absolutely nothing about seminars, took it over; they thought that I knew how, but I didn't. That was a difficult week, and so was the week after. He went back to the hospital one day for intravenous feeding, which I now realize we could have had at home. Then after that he was fine. Until later on.

He could write almost anywhere without being disturbed. I don't think that has much to do with self-hypnosis, but with his habit of studying since he was a child, wherever he was. Noise would not bother him much.

People very much had that image of him [as aloof]. I think that it was true, but it was true in the past. Whether because he was older or because of the psychedelic drugs or because of changes in his life, I saw shadows of that but I didn't ever see the real thing; only because I'm more impatient. I was much more impatient than he was; he had tremendous patience. He would always say, "Oh, wait, wait."

Juliette Huxley (sister-in-law)

The frightening thing is that he knew he had cancer. He'd had this operation of the tongue, which was cured with radium needles, not surgery. He then had the growth in his throat. And when he came back from Sweden in 1963 [he came go visit me], he looked very, very gray. His face was frightening. He was also weak. I thought the American doctors weren't doing him any good, so I got an appointment at Bart's Hospital, with very good doctors. And I said to him, "Aldous, I'm taking you to Bart's Hospital for a consultation."

"Oh, why?" He looked rather surprised and angry. I said, "Well, you don't look well, and I think our doctors are very good in England." He didn't discuss it. He said, "All right."

I put him in the car and drove him down to Bart's. I waited behind the door, of course. He came out, got back in the car, and then he said, "Well, they think it's just a bad cold I've got—a bad infection, and I'll get over it."

All this time he knew he was dying of cancer, but he did not want to tell us. And we were blind and stupid enough not to guess from his looks what he had. He really looked gray and was evidently very weak—something more serious than a cold. I felt, I can't discuss it. *He* obviously didn't want to discuss it. He told Laura that he had a very bad fright when I took him to the hospital, because he thought the truth would come out. But you see, the doctors never told me what they thought. He said to them:

"I know I'm dying, and I know my sister-in-law and my brother [are] worried about me, but I know my illness and you can't do anything about it. She insisted on bringing me here, but it's no help at all. Thank you very much." And he walked out, you see.

Laura Huxley (writer, second wife)

Aldous knew he was dying, but he didn't speak about it. I have spoken of this in my book *[This Timeless Moment]*. I cannot say it's all wrong, but when I read it I was surprised.

I remember one time that he drank two whiskey and sodas. It was strange. We were coming back from New York when he was really ill. We went to consult an oncologist who told me this was it; [Aldous] was very bad. I do not remember everything; that was sometime in the spring of 1963. I don't know how much he knew about what the doctor had said (the doctor hadn't said anything to him directly) but it was the doctor that our Dr. Cutler wanted us to go and see. We just stayed there, one night, and came back. On the way back, on the trip, he ordered a whiskey and soda and I think he had two. It was very funny; he became very high. He was very courtly, very charming.

The last few months were difficult. He was not in pain; he was just feeling the same. It was not even his mood— he acted as usual, but he looked down. I was worried.

When he was finally dying, he gave me a note that said, "LSD, 100 micrograms." I had given him injections all the time during that period, because he was taking Dilaudid, a morphine. During the last three weeks, whenever he needed it, I gave him the injections, whenever he needed vitamins and other things. I injected the LSD in his arm.

There was a lot of unrest in the morning. A doctor was giving him some kind of special injection in the bronchial tubes. He was sitting up. I did not know a thing about that, but that was seemingly what they were doing. Then he said, "I can't take this any longer."

Evidently it was very painful. In the morning, there was a sort of restlessness, as if he did not know what to do. I did not know what to do. Then, when he gave me the prescription, I knew. It was clear. It always had been like that. He would come to a decision quite quickly, and then the decision was gone.

Timothy Leary came here when Aldous was dying. I remember very well; he came to visit with a beautiful woman. Then he wrote that Aldous told him that he was dying, but I did not know it, and I told him that Aldous was dying, but he did not know it. Really, that [scene] is not correct.

Rosalind Rajagopal (friend)

All I know is, I was with him the day he died. That has a great deal of meaning for me. Because I knew I was with a very remarkable person and a wonderful presence. After all, I loved him very much, but not a tear. It was just a beautiful passing and a beautiful everything, the whole atmosphere, the whole thing. Whether anybody else felt this or not, I don't know. Laura was in and out and the woman that lived there [Ginny Pfeiffer]; but I stayed the whole day, every minute. Well, I'm going to tell you about myself.

I had certain days I would go to Hollywood, and that was understood. And this was not one of those days. I woke up with a terrific feeling, "I've just got to go down; I've got to go down." I said [to my friend], "Dr. Jordan, I have this terrific feeling, I've got to go down to see Aldous." They were friends. He said, "Go." I said, "What do you think I should do?" He said, "I think you should go." There was one or two things that needed to be done in Ojai that could be done in Hollywood, and [he] said I could do those down there. I went, and I got as far as my little house on Dora Street. There were men working on the street. I would never turn up at somebody's house without letting them know. They said, "Did you hear that Kennedy was shot?" I said, "No, I haven't heard anything." I wanted to go in and telephone. So I went into the house stairs to telephone Laura, and said, "I'm here, can I come to see Aldous?" She said, "Come right away, come right away." She said, "Come. Hurry."

So I went downstairs and the men said that Kennedy had been shot; they heard on the radio. So, I went up a few blocks to their house, and I went in, and Maria [sic] said the doctor had said they shouldn't tell him anything about Kennedy. I don't think anything we would have told him would have made any difference. Anyway, he was all there mentally, and he had tummy aches. I'd never done his tummy before, but I always did his hands or feet to make him feel well. And he said, "Would you rub my tummy?" And when I did, he didn't like that. It didn't help him at all. Nothing helped him. So, he sat there, and he said, "Well, rock the bed," which I did. Laura had done that, too, but she was in and out. He was worried about papers. What was it? An insurance paper, I think it was, that should be signed, and Laura said it wasn't there. Then it was there; it had come.

So, I was watching that; because I thought here she told

him it wasn't there and I saw it was there, and she didn't let him sign it. Afterwards, she saw the insurance did go to Matthew, so we don't need to say anything wrong about that. But, anyway, I sat there with him the whole day, and there was an extraordinary feeling of greatness. I don't know, I can't explain it. It was just peaceful and beautiful and actually wonderful. Now, I had never been with a person dying before, and you ordinarily feel like weeping, but I didn't feel like weeping, I just felt exhilarated, just extraordinary.

The real doctor that he had was in Riverside, and there was a substitute doctor, and a Negro nurse, and she was very nice. When they went into this thing about LSD, there was a doctor there because I said to him, "Is it all right?" He said, "It doesn't matter what they do now." He said he didn't care; let them give him anything. But Aldous asked for it, I must say. And when he went, you didn't know he had died; he just passed off quietly.

Chapter VI
His Legacy and Critical
Reception Today

At the end of June, 1994, a few weeks short of Aldous Huxley's centenary, scholars from the United States, Europe, and Asia gathered in Munster Germany to debate the author's legacy.

The papers of the Aldous Huxley Centenary Symposium concerned newly uncovered texts, his critical reception, his philosophical failings. Yet by the final session, on the ethical responsibilities of Huxley's biographers and critics, I wondered at the many different personae of Huxley which we had heard. Walls seemed to divide the epochs of his life, his fiction from his essays or poetry, his older readers from his younger ones. Contemplating these divisions, I recalled the response of art critic and novelist John Berger to the ethical obligations of writers.

All of us live inside walls of our own experience and time. Inside, we go about our business and our pursuit of pleasure; and after a while we don't even notice the walls at all. The writer's responsibility is to awaken readers to a passioante possibility, to remind us that there is a life outside. That the prejudices of now and here are small and passing, compared to what lies just beyond reach.

Or, as Calamy says at the end of Huxley's *Those Barren*

Leaves, "There is a reality which is totally different and which a change would enable us to get nearer to . . . perhaps if you spend long enough and your mind is the right sort, perhaps you really do get beyond the limitations of ordinary existence." Perhaps, and now more than ever.

What follows is an overview of what today's critics are saying and writing about Huxley. This is obviously not the first symposium of critics on Huxley. Among the notable predecessors were the above-mentioned symposium of *London Magazine;* the testimonies of prominent intellectuals such as Isaiah Berlin in the memorial volume edited by Julian Huxley[1]; and a 1974 critical collection edited by Robert Kuehn.[2]

Of the two dozen scholars on the symposium program, eight were interviewed for this chapter; these are some—by no means all—of the world's leading authorities on Huxley, people who together have written dozens of essays, reviews, and books on the author. Though critics and literary historians often disagree on Huxley's work, in the pages that follow we find considerable agreement about key issues in Huxley's critical reception today: what his work means to today's readers; which are the most important works, and how might they be understood; which incidents in Huxley's life and work require further study (such as the roles of his women characters); and which works of his deserve reexamination. (The proceedings of the symposium are to be published by Peter Verlag, a German publisher, in 1995.)

Our first section begins with suggestions on where the modern reader of Huxley might start reading—with and beyond *Brave New World.*

Phillip Thody (University of Leeds)

I think that the best novel, as a novel from a purely formal point of view, is *Crome Yellow.* It's the novel in which he has the greatest control over his material, it has the shaped framed narrative of the man who's small and whose son grows to be a giant, it has some of the wittiest conversation, and it is one in which all points of view are presented effectively (because with equal irony).

However, if I had to say to somebody, I think there's one book you should read by Huxley after *Brave New World,* I think it would be *Point Counter Point,* which explores his sense of the tragic contradictions in the human tradition. I think there is a difference between the Huxley up to and perhaps including *Eyeless in Gaza,* 1936, and the Huxley after the self-imposed exile to North America in April 1937, accompanied if you remember by the remark that he made on stepping on board ship, "Europe is no place for a pacifist."

Some qualities of the early Huxley remain in the later American Huxley. I think that, for example, *Ape and Essence,* which is a very dramatic and very effective vision of a dystopia in the future, a dystopia of a different kind from *Brave New World,* is extremely effective. I also think that the plotting of both *Time Must Have a Stop* and *After Many a Summer* is excellent. It's simply that I would eliminate Mr. Propter from after *Many a Summer* and I think I would eliminate Bruno Rontini from *Time.*

The other novel that I would recommend people to read is *Eyeless in Gaza* if only because of the depiction of the child's grief at the death of the parent, and also because of the technique in narration which did in a more understandable and accessible manner what Faulkner had done some years earlier in *The Sound and the Fury.*

Peter Firchow (University of Minnesota)

My own favorite Huxley novel is *Eyeless in Gaza.* It's a very difficult work technically. I think possibly some of the fireworks of the technique, of the mix-up of dates and so on, is just that—showing off that Huxley can do what all those other modernist folks did. But underneath that surface there is a really genuine concern with the issues: a paradigmatic life of a person, an intellectual again, someone who is emotionally impaired, finding his way to his emotions, finding his way to other people. Like so many works that are very broad, it may be off-putting at first. But remember when you meet an interesting person you may be off-put by that person at first, and you've got to stick it out for a while.

I realize that other people felt an absence, a lack; that there was some part of Huxley that just wasn't there, that he was missing something that was very important. I think he realizes that himself. So much of his fiction is about that lack of emotional strength, emotional commitment. I think he's also very skeptical about it.

A number of his characters, especially women characters, are versions of Frieda Lawrence, and clearly he senses that the intellectual male needs some kind of a strong, emotionally confident female to help him. Sometimes I begin to think that the emotional female becomes even more important than the male.

Jerome Meckier (University of Kentucky)

If people liked *Brave New World* (I mean by that probably if they were appalled by it), they might want to read the antidote, so to speak, Huxley wrote thirty years later: *Island,* the other side of the coin. If *Brave New World* is a synthesis of all the possible things that could go wrong in society, *Island* is Huxley's last attempt to put together all the possible positive things that could happen to us.

Island and some of the work that Huxley wrote about his own experiments with drugs [and meditation], such as *The Doors of Perception,* or *Heaven and Hell,* show you the man on his spiritual pilgrimage. They were very timely then, I think they still have some relevance now.

[What work is least appreciated or understood?] One could look at the least-known of his novels, *The Genius and the Goddess,* or one could look at the least popular of his three futuristic novels, *Ape and Essence.* My ultimate choice would be *The Perennial Philosophy,* which is an anthology of mystical writings, spliced together in a way, a much more serious work in his career than most people would have appreciated to this point.

I have a first edition of *The Perennial Philosophy* and whoever the person was who owned it wrote in the margin, "This is a pretentious fake." I don't think it's a fake, I don't think it's pretentious.

Guin Nance (Auburn University)

The last conversations with my students about Huxley, some were steering away from *Time Must Have a Stop*, that's a book that I think is worthy of some exploration but is difficult in a lot of ways. *Antic Hay* was one that my students started with some skepticism and ended I think with great interest, and also found it profoundly funny at times. Another was *Point Counter Point* that they rather became enthralled with; and since they were also looking at Lawrence, they found *PCP* a nice entrée.

While critics have their individual favorites for works to engage the interest of the next generation of Huxley students and scholars, most agree on the central works of a Huxley canon—a necessary step in analyzing an author who wrote so many books. In the next pages, the panel of scholars outlines the importance of key works. Any such reckoning includes classics such as *Brave New World, Crome Yellow, Antic Hay, Point Counter Point, Eyeless in Gaza, After Many a Summer, Doors of Perception,* and *Island.* Yet other works deserve particular attention for the issues or eras they reflect: *Ends and Means* and *Science, Liberty and Peace,* for those studying the pacifist, communitarian Huxley; *Ape and Essence,* for those studying the American years and the utopian/dystopian tradition; *The Perennial Philosophy,* for those interested in the mystic Huxley; and *Grey Eminence,* for those interested in Huxley as a biographer.

Brave New World will always be in the forefront of any critical consideration of Aldous Huxley. Not only is it the work of his most widely read and one that contains so many topical concerns—such as the difficulty of living a decent life in a mass-culture world—but it also forecasts the author's later concern with drugs, hypnosis, and the United States.

Similarly, *Island,* Huxley's last novel—and the one to which he returned for his trademark blend of essayistic exposition and narrative—emerges as an encyclopedia of Huxley's preoccupations of his later years. (And because a comprehensive text has yet to be published).

Kirpal Singh (Nanyang Technological University)

In *Brave New World* he does clearly signal Freud and the pleasure principle versus the reality principle; Huxley is saying that in the long term, it's the pleasure principle that's going to be the most dangerous weapon by which human intelligence will be retarded and thwarted.

The warning is that if we are not careful it is not brute, savage power that is going to be our next oppressor but it is going to be the world of quick consumerism, quick chemical sensationalism, and quick jingoism.

James Sexton (Camosun College)

The genesis of the play *Now More Than Ever,* as I can determine from the letters, was July of '32. He had just written *Brave New World.* Huxley was writing to his father in July 1932, talking about how he was beginning a play based on some of the economic problems of the day. The economic crisis in 1931. The play was finished by October of 1932, and what fascinates me is the interlinked quality of the works from, say *Brave New World,* which was written in '31, published in '32, so essentially the same time frame. Along with some unnoticed articles under the rubric "Abroad in England" three months in a row in Nash's *Pall Mall* magazine. They appeared from May through July 1931, and a fourth, "Greater and Lesser London: Snapshots of Men About Town" in October. Now all of these works deal with the problems of economic drift and Huxley's concerns with perhaps even the Achilles' heel of capitalism, i.e., the greed of entrepreneurs.

The person who had the success [with drama] was Christopher Isherwood, and I believe that a great deal of Huxley's persistence in trying to come up with a successful vehicle was based on his wish to emulate the success of Isherwood with *I Am a Camera,* which apparently brought Isherwood a great deal of money.

One of the major contradictions or paradoxes in *Brave New World* is the fact that the powers described as tyrannical are capitalists, bureaucrats, or tyrannical commissars: *"Plus ça change; plus c'est la même chose."* The capitalist essence *is* the communist essence; big capitalism *is* big communism, state capitalism espoused later on by Lenin, continued by Stalin by the love affair with American capitalists like Henry Ford and the time and motion expert F. W. Taylor, enshrining this capitalistic movement, is the central paradox; they became one in their ultimate concern with mechanization and productivity at all costs.

Phillip Thody

My ideas on *Brave New World* have rather been changed, as one of the great advantages of coming to this conference. I had thought of it as being an entirely satirical work, in other words, that Huxley was denouncing the dangers of a society that was dominated entirely by reason and science. That he was saying that man could attain the kind of happiness in *Brave New World* only by ceasing to be human, because you give up loving, you give up art, you give up philosophy, you give up science (in anything but the sense of applied science), and then you are happy. So you start being happy by stopping being human. This was a straightforward ethical and philosophical dilemma, and I think that is one of the features that makes *Brave New World* perhaps the best of all science fiction novels, because it asks a fundamental metaphysical question.

Now what I discovered yesterday was that it's also in a

sense a self-criticism on Huxley's part, because in the years preceding its publication, Huxley was in fact arguing precisely in favor of the creation of scientific society, in which science would take over, in which democracy would be dispensed with, in the cause of the greater efficiency, and that he was also arguing in favor of eugenic engineering.

Most of the students to whom I've talked about *Brave New World* have confessed to me that they first of all read it because it depicted what you might call an adolescent's utopia, that everybody could have everybody else without any fear of consequences because contraception was highly effective; venereal disease seemed to have been abolished; and much of the appeal of the early Huxley lay to the highly sexed but irreverent adolescent who was tired of the sexual repression inculcated by his schoolmasters and his parents, terrified of having sex with members of the opposite sex because of having babies, and thought that in fact that Huxley's dystopia was in fact something of a utopia.

I happened to look at the centenary edition of *Antic Hay,* and I saw that it had a preface by David Lodge (probably the most interesting novelist writing in English today). And Lodge's reaction to this was almost exactly the same as mine. That is, here you had intellectuals talking about exciting ideas, they were leading interesting lives, it was totally different from the suburban repressive mediocracy in which you were being brought up.

I think that the excitement of the ideas is doubled in Huxley by a realization of the ultimate tragedy of human existence, which is that human beings have to live an animal existence on human terms. We know we are going to die, we might well have very nasty diseases like cancers; perhaps what is even more, we might see people we love have a nasty disease called cancer. (This is the ultimate horror of physical disease and unmerited death of the innocent that is embodied in the death of Little Phil in *Point Counter Point.*) It's the combination of the excitement of ideas and this deep awareness of the tragedy of human existence that makes Huxley still a very exciting author, perhaps in a tradition that is more continental than English. For me, it is quite a natural transition to move from reading Huxley to reading Malraux, Sartre, and Camus.

Guin Nance

I still am rather enchanted by his first novel [Crome Yellow], and I find that some undergraduates are as well. It's a period piece in some ways, and yet still a kind of a charming book that adumbrates some later Huxley ideas.

I like Eyeless in Gaza; but not all critics do. Many critics fault the chronological sequencing and find the book too long and worthy of cutting. I think Huxley's doing interesting things with memory and how we, to use a Wordsworthian phrase, bind our days together.

Island always tantalizes because you know what hopes Huxley placed in the novel in his sense of trying to bring it all together in the last book.

Phillip Thody

There was the feeling that like Auden and Isherwood (who you remember are satirized in Evelyn Waugh's Put Out More Flags in the characters of the twin poets Parsnip and Pimpernel) that you ought not to leave your native country in a difficult time. That perhaps the attitude of Henry James, who took on British citizenship in 1915, was the correct attitude for an author to accept. That, of course, is the kind of remark that would immediately lay me open to a good deal of criticism on the ground of being a nationalist. But I think that it is understandable that English people should have felt a bit reserved about him, but obviously there wasn't anything he could do if he'd have stayed. He wasn't of military age, he'd been declared unfit for military service in 1914, so perhaps he did the right thing, because it did enable him to keep on writing books.

I am in something of a minority among the people who are gathered here today since I am not an ecologist and I am not a pacifist, I'm a profoundly conservative, conventional, middle-class English skeptic. And I think that many of the statements made about Huxley's ideas are as [P. G. Wodehouse's character] Jeeves said of Nietzsche, "fundamentally unsound." I don't think you could possibly organize a society on the lines that Huxley sets out in *Island* and I don't think that his ideas on politics have any value whatsoever. His value for me is in the sense that he wrote extremely exciting, extremely irreverent novels.

Kirpal Singh

Brave New World is a text with commentary. It's read in schools. The conference inspired me to read the later Huxley, because what I read of *Island:* there Huxley seemed to search for a new kind of lifestyle and lifeform and a new kind of utopia; whereas in *Brave New World* it is an antiutopia . . . I am more interested in the *positive* utopia that could be possible although I heard that utopia in the beautiful paradiselike situation has finally destroyed an island, but still I am interested what he thought a modern society would be like and so I think I am going to re-read *Island.*

I am third generation Sikh Singaporan, basically educated in English from about the age of four; I did my Ph.D. in Adelaide, Australia. My basic interest in Huxley is a thinker that tries to reconcile some of the apparent irreconcilables, what I consider very deep-seated attitudinal differences between East and West.

If there is one text [my students read] I would say *Island.* They enjoy reading *Brave New World,* but very often it could boil down to a titter and a twitter. *Island* they really take seriously. Because he offers a vision of the future. More significantly, it offers a vision of the future which is perverted and ultimately destroyed by a very subtle intrusion of what in Asia we are quite worried about even today. The ultimate destruction of Pala by the big oil corporations in cahoots with the corrupt locals is something that we are very conscious of in the politics of our everyday life.

Bernfried Nugel (Westphalia University)

At the beginning [in the writing of *Island*] there was this fine feeling on Huxley's part that he had finished his novel after a long course of revisions in the beginning of June 1961, and sent off two copies to the British and American publishers each; and then he thought, well, this is definitive, or final version of *Island*.

And then the editors of his British and American publishers, they got together behind his back and said, "Well, this novel is just too long, it's too much, it contains too much exposition for the love of the exposition." They would have to put it to Huxley to make cuts. And they did it in a very, say humanitarian way that didn't confront Huxley with a decision: well, we leave it in your hands; perhaps you could—might—do something about it.

When Huxley came to London—just two weeks after he had sent in the manuscript, imagine that—he sat down and took up revisions again, although he had been revising the whole thing for years, you see [laughs]. Amazing, really. He cut out, if I could calculate, let's say fifty or so typescript pages.

If you relook at the passages, I think they are of extreme importance to the general structure of the book. I wouldn't call it a novel, I wouldn't call it a satire, I wouldn't call it a utopia. This is his dilemma: well, should he write a novel with a plot, and if he did, how could he integrate the philosophical aspects or ideas he had?

[What's in the missing pages of *Island*?] First of all, he made extensive cuts in the notes on *What's What*, the book that the old Raj, one of the founders of Pala, wrote; it contains the underlying principles of Raja himself. I argue that these notes *What's What* were a carefully structured philosophical essay in the final version of *Island* that Huxley sent to the publishers; but after he commits such immense cuts, they may appear incoherent or even cryptic in some parts. You could argue they are quite redundant, but you could argue it's the style of the old Raja, it's the Oriental style, that Huxley tries to imitate there.

He cut passages in the narration proper, containing plot elements and characterization. He cut dialogue passages as well, dialogue being the most lively way of integrating philosophical thoughts in Huxley's own terms. Readers may feel that there are too many abrupt transitions, no real argument in many places, just a collection of aphorisms; in Chapter 11 Huxley reduced some ten pages into one sentence, an aphorism.

Kirpal Singh

There is, I think, an Asian perspective on Huxley. To regard Huxley purely as a novelist and accuse him of failure from a very limited perspective that decides even before it is willing to accept a new novel, that this is what a novel should be, is wrong. That judgment should come after you open yourselves up to the experience rather than before you approach the experience, that's the gulf between the Eastern critics and the Western critics.

I think all Asians would be very interested in the way others see us, and the way others use us. Now we have been seen and used by certainly the white peoples of the world for centuries and many of us are so colonized that we are totally willing to endorse what the white critic says about Huxley even before we ourselves experience it.

Peter Firchow

I wrote my dissertation on Huxley in 1965. I'd always been skeptical of people who devote their lives to just one writer. It seemed to me that they were tempted too much to become a version of that writer, and I didn't want to have that happen to me. I said [to myself], I've done my book, I'll never do anything on Huxley again. Of course that wasn't true. I immediately proceeded to write a whole slew of articles on Huxley, mostly having to do with the relation of science and literature and the arts generally. Most humanists feel sort of inferior in the presence of scientists. I think Huxley said when he got in the presence of scientists he felt like a peasant in the company of dukes. So, in a lesser way I felt that way, too.

Both [his fiction and his nonfiction] are very powerful. The fiction is ultimately more satisfying because it's broader—especially the short fiction is more brilliant, more intriguing, more immediately appealing. The essays, the discursive writing, has a power that is pretty absent in the fiction because it presents you with Huxley as a kind of interlocutor that seems to take responsibility for what's being said in a way that you don't get in the fiction. So there's an immediate relationship with the voice that's speaking to you through his essays.

Jerome Meckier

I am very much interested in his intellectual and artistic development inasmuch as they furnish a paradigm I think for the modern period, for the modern consciousness. Watching the man develop from a cynical, irreverent, satirical writer of considerable skill to a probing would-be or aspiring mystic person looking for answers to the purpose or point of life is a very impressive spectacle to try and study and understand.

Based on the written works, it would seem to me that he was always a very capable student or scholar of religious awareness or expanded awareness and that he got to the threshold of the breakthrough he was looking for. And perhaps no further. But this is again a considerable achievement.

Pierre Vitoux (University of Montpellier)

The later novels were not very well received in France. If you ask any Frenchmen, "Huxley, what does that mean to you?" He'll almost always answer *Brave New World, Point Counter Point.*

Guin Nance

Some of Huxley's female types are the Siren or what I'm calling the Dragon, a sort of man-eater woman (characterized best by Myra Viviash and Lucy Tantamount in *Point Counter Point*, or Mary Amberly in *Eyeless in Gaza*. Another type, often comic, in the Huxley novels is the virgin, she is sometimes portrayed positively in a light comedy and sometimes satirically, as in the superannuated virgin of *Point Counter Point*, Beatrice Gilray. The most positive types are two really: the Dragoman (or interpreter) in *Point Counter Point* of which Elinor Quarles is prototypic. When we get to *Island*, a much more fully delineated guide or interpreter or revealer would be Susila, who leads [the protagonist] Will Farnaby through a psychic journey towards healing in a much more substantial sense than Elinor is a dragoman for Philip Quarles.

Another type is what I'm calling the instinctual woman (Mary Rampion, in *Point Counter Point*, and more fully, later in Katie Martins in *The Genius and the Goddess*) a woman whom Huxley very clearly links with Mother Nature, life force. A woman who has the force of life within her, as he describes it, and is not able to reach that third state of grace that Huxley envisioned for *Island*, but still is a very important demarcation on the way.

Huxley was prone to use what he knew, and in that case, would be women he had known. In the earliest novel, *Crome Yellow*, we see a good bit of Lady Ottoline Morrell in the Priscilla Wimbush figure with her house party and her odd assortments of people on the weekends and her interest in horoscopes and collection of sometimes young men as well. Later, the two most notable characterizations of real-life women would be Frieda Lawrence (as Katie Martins in *The Genius and the Goddess*). And in that strange, bubble-headed woman in *After Many a Summer*, Virginia Maunciple, probably lies a Marian Davies prototype.

I think Huxley starts with a natural antipathy for the physiological aspects of love, so I think he brings that to it as much from his own perspective as attributing it to woman as sort of the vessels as we get in *Ape and Essence*. There's that idyllic, almost-romance, with Irene and Lord Hovenden in *Those Barren Leaves*, which doesn't have the under-cutting satire or the rather distasteful, to use my word, physical descriptions that indicate Huxley, while he obviously sees sexuality as a natural part of human life, finds it rather ridiculous and sometimes disgusting. I guess it's the Swiftian element we've all commented on in the Huxley world. His idealistic young men, I think most typically, have both, are both attracted to, obviously, sexuality, and have a kind of revulsion afterwards. But I wouldn't want to lay the blame entirely on the women; although there are some who initiate idealistic young men into sexuality. You can look at them as women vamps leading the man on, or you can look at them as more real-life women with hormones, who initiate young men into a broader view of sexuality.

He has a kind of moralist revulsion at times against sexuality. Indications are that he personally liked it, but it seems that every once in a while the moralist comes out and he has a second-thought revulsion.

What's interesting to me in *Island*, the Palinese practice of sex aside, is the Farnaby-Susula relationship: near the end, Farnaby clearly has a sexual feeling for Susula and wants to sleep with her. But rather than follow that urge, he sees the wisdom of holding back in a way that's positive for once in Huxley. Farnaby's learning something about emotion deeper than pure sexuality; Huxley is allowing that to happen.

Interest in Huxley, critical and biographical, seems to arrive in waves. The first of these might be England's preoccupation with the bright young poet and satirist, who was a figure marked for distinction by the time he was twenty-five. A second phase of interest occurs in the late 1930s and war years, as Huxley was appraised by those who had heralded

him earlier for shifting praxis of his fiction toward the peda-
gogic and away from a cultural nihilism. There followed a
lull lasted almost into the 1960s, at which point *Doors of
Perception* and *Perennial Philosophy* appealed to a new generation of readers. Then in the 1960s and '70s, particularly
after his death, a number of retrospective analyses of his
career appeared; and then another lull. In the late 1980s and
1990s, another wave may have emerged, influenced by post-
modern literary theorists who claim Huxley for their number,
biographers working in a more candid time, literary historians
seeking more and more complete texts.

Such currents inevitably affect (and are affected by) shifts
in the dominant culture. In twenty years, we may well see
another wave, interested in Huxley not as a novelist or icon
for post-World War I disaffection but as a health *savant* open
to the psychological dimensions of healing and the psychic
capacities of human intelligence. None can say which side of
Huxley will draw the next adherents—or if he will vanish
from the literary-intellectual horizon altogether.

In the interim before some more final critical assessment of
Huxley's place in twentieth-century letters, it may be thought-
provoking to consider pending biographical questions, such
as those discussed in the Introduction or below. What if Huxley had been fully sighted all his life? If he had discovered
his cancer earlier and he had lived into the 1980s? If he had
won the Nobel Prize?

What might Huxley have written if he had remained in
England? If he had tempered his affinity for pacifism and
embraced the war against Fascism and Nazism?

Pierre Vitoux

In the interval of the war, Huxley had been forgotten or
at least [there] had been this kind of interlude. Suddenly
on rediscovering him we found that he had changed completely, that what he stood for was different.

Phillip Thody

Now it is arguable that he might have written rather better books if he had stayed in England. Huxley obviously got some good material by going to California. I think that *After Many a Summer* is absolutely hilarious from that point of view. The account of the visit to Joe Stoye's castle, obviously identifiable with the Castle Encantada of W. H. Hearst, the newspaper magnate, and perhaps we should be grateful to Huxley for having written about America. He might, however, have written a very interesting book about England in wartime.

I don't think it was a question of [the British] not forgiving Aldous. Yet he's not normally taught in English universities, whereas Lawrence is.

Guin Nance

[If Huxley had lived longer] I think his view of women probably would have evolved into a more contemporary view, I think he would have continued to have been fascinated and continued his thinking about ecological issues about which he was really a forerunner. I think the whole question of nationalism is of some concern, again something he thought about a long time ago and would still be writing about I'm sure. The interesting thing about Huxley is that he did keep learning and he continued to be fascinated by those ideas.

Kirpal Singh

I see Huxley as a very significant bridge [between East and West]. I don't think that bridge has been successfully built yet, but I think Huxley attempted to build a bridge more holistic than most of the others before him. I am also thinking of people from the East who try to do the same kind of bridging, like Radnakrishna and Tagore; but I think Huxley came closest so far.

There is a kind of irony contained in his remarks on the

East; it is not exactly very flattering if one reads it carefully, nor is it flattering to Americans. There's a long way away from 1915–1916 when Huxley the Etonian, the Oxfordian, and 1963 when he died: a long journey. The man who thought he was something, could realize he was in fact nothing, and then he realized again that he could be something.

Peter Firchow

One of the reasons why he went to America was because he was no longer the same man. He realized that, as Auden did when he went to America, too, that there was something different about him that America might satisfy. I think of the Lawrence of *St. Mawr* who has the novel end in the mountains of New Mexico [as Huxley did in *Brave New World*]. That's the place where Huxley went, too; there was something more real, closer to the heart of nature, in America, despite all the superficiality and consumerism. He could get close to reality there; at least he hoped to.

He saw British society as something that was really basically provincial, that didn't address the main issues of the time, that was completely self-absorbed. If he was going to make a step beyond what he was, a brilliant satirist, somebody who saw the faults of society and lashed them, he would miss an opportunity; he would be false to what I think he recognized was his true mission, namely to dig deeper, to see more, to recognize some of the really basic truths of our existence that have to do with the basic needs of people: hunger, sex, death [laughs].

Jerome Meckier

[Why was Huxley drawn to drugs?] By a rather scientific instinct. I think he believed that drugs should be kept away from all the people except those who might benefit the most from them; people who were intellectually, philosophically prepared to see what sort of enlargement of consciousness the drugs might bring. I know he and Timothy Leary, for example, had a big falling out about it. LSD was not a new religion, it was something to be used very sparingly, very carefully, and I think that Aldous himself used it—very experimentally, if you like.

Huxley is not a "flower child," he is not a person who would have been hanging out in the Haight-Ashbury; though he would not have been adverse to talking to those people and sharing his experiences with them, but that's not the direction he himself would have taken.

[Why were Lawrence and Huxley drawn to each other?] You have a working-class, miner's child and a man with a First from Oxford; and they must have looked at each other like they were from two different planets. Yet surprisingly, they both had this desire to answer the riddle of why we are alive or how we should live. This may have been the ultimate bond between them. They seem to have been very good friends—arguably Huxley is Lawrence's last and longest friend as his premature death approaches. The differences between them remained very strong but the *bond*, the desire for a new, and a more rewarding way to live is what kept them together.

One of the early efforts I remember making as a writer was to try and scotch the two Huxley theories. The idea that there was the satirist and then there came the saint. To me the saint is implicit in the satirist and the satirist still lives in the saint. Huxley initially spoke to the postwar World War I generation; his cynicism, his skepticism was a real breath of fresh air for them, a real liberating influence. Then, as you might put it vulgarly, when he got religion, a lot of these people were very very disappointed, feeling that they had been betrayed. Here's a man who told them that the point of everything was pointlessness and now he was telling them there was a point to it all, after all. It must have been somewhat confusing and disappointing. During the 1930s, Huxley loses a lot of readers. But this is a man who lost readers and got new readers and regained old readers all his life. He has had more lives than a cat intellectually and I think that will continue.

A final question for any literary history is why we should read the author's works today: a combination of literary style and personal panache, of topicality and timelessness, repays the time and effort to engage a mind more capacious than one's own. As Professor Nugel and others comment in the next pages, Huxley is rarely an easy read for today's readers, conditioned by our easy access to mass-entertainment devices. His frame of reference requires an historical and anthropological breadth found in few modern liberal arts graduates; he rarely bothers translating or identifying his allusions; and, for an audience used to the conventions of popular literature, his discursiveness poses near-insurmountable barriers.

Yet the scholars here provide reasons why Huxley is (and should be) read. For some, reading Huxley is akin to playing mental chess; for others he is an oracle consulted at different points on life's journey. A few want him as soothsayer for the next century; some, less enthralled by his social and educational dicta, feel he is worth reading as a link to the literary traditions of the Victorian and Edwardian eras.

Whichever the reader chooses, Huxley is clearly many things to many people. I must conclude that Huxley would have embraced this polytheist approach to his own importance, as in these lines he quoted from Shelley in *Texts and Pretexts:*

> I never was attached to that great sect,
> Whose doctrine is that each one should
> > select
> Out of the crowd a mistress or a friend,
> And all the rest, though fair and wise,
> > commend
> To cold oblivion . . .

James Sexton

We should read Huxley, the prose writer, today because of his ongoing concern with problems that still vex humanity. One of them, of course, is ecological destruction. We have Huxley the theorist about war, about the problems that result from nationalism. The issues that Huxley dealt with have, of course, not been solved; his whole life was devoted to dealing with the Problems that require Solutions, the big problems, and I think that perhaps more than most writers his concerns are still with us.

Bernfried Nugel

[Why read him today?] Well, it's not a question of reading him today, it's a question of not having read him earlier than today, and it's a question of reading him in the future. We should read him today to be able to read him in the right way in the future, and something has got to be done to read him in the proper texts would be the first thing. We need critical texts.

Huxley is a demanding writer; he's not just a writer whom you can read in your bed when you go to sleep and then try to dream happily. This is one of his favorite aphorisms of course, "Patriotism is not enough, Science is not enough, Philosophy is not enough, whatever you have is not enough, nothing short of everything will do."

Huxley's essays are not so easy to read, they demand a cultural (or at least literary) background in the reader, and this is, of course, one of the main problems for reading Huxley; you must have arrived at a certain stage where you can really relish Huxley's immense knowledge and his superiority over the reader. You must be strong enough to stand that; but if you do, you have a good opinion of yourself; because you say, well, now I have in a sense tried to match such a polymath.

Phillip Thody

I would have thought Huxley would still be worth reading a century from now in the way that an author such as George Eliot is still being read because he is in one of the traditions of the English novel, a confrontation of different points of view. I don't think that anyone in English literature departments would accept the comparison between *Middlemarch* and *Point Counter Point,* because they would say it was rather like comparing *King Lear* to *My Fair Lady.*

Kirpal Singh

My daughters would read Huxley partly because I think they realize their daddy was influenced by Huxley to an extent which they have to come to terms with. Another reason is that Huxley in a very true sense does try to at least attempt a prescription. I don't think his attempt is totally successful. The world is not always very comfortable with the smug successes of minor figures but with the colossal failures of colossals.

Peter Firchow

Today very few people—relative to the total population—read anything at all except newspapers or magazines. But among that population of people who read books, there are always going to be people who will want to read Huxley because he, like Lawrence or Hermann Hesse, especially provides answers to very pressing questions people have. They may be answers that may eventually strike you as absurd and wrong, but at a certain stage in one's life I think they appeal immensely.

The main question is the overwhelming question that we all face, what's the meaning of life? And how should I go about living it? And how do I make basic decisions about whom do I love, whom do I associate with, why do I do it?

Huxley has both the strength and the weakness of addressing these big questions, and that's clearly why he appeals to audiences in Central Europe and Eastern Europe who are used to writers who ask those questions and doesn't appeal to people in the Anglo-Saxon tradition who by and large tend to feel that such questions are—how shall I say it—things that should not be asked too publicly.

There will always be a small group, even fifty years from

now, maybe even a hundred years from now [devoted to Huxley]; it depends on whether any of us are still around, in terms of the human species. When he said that only one tenth of one percent of the population of the world is the audience or even the source of the characters that he has in *Point Counter Point,* he is probably being pretty accurate.

On the other hand, these are problems of that one tenth of one percent, and that tends to be the one tenth of one percent that makes things happen in the world. Therefore it's very important to understand those. You can learn from Huxley how to add to mental excess a balance of emotion and appreciation of the senses.

Guin Nance

[In Huxley] you see this vast panorama of ideas and times and places envisioned by a man of great intellect—and great humor at times. He is indeed serious and ponderous at times in his exposition. But there's the comic element in him as well. The following of a mind that's quick and lively is just one of the pleasures of reading Huxley.

Jerome Meckier

[What do people today know of Huxley?] If they've been through the American educational system, they are probably thinking of the author of *Brave New World.* If they are a generation older than myself, they are probably thinking of some of the novels that Huxley wrote in the postwar period; maybe they know *Point Counter Point,* or some of the earlier comic novels from the twenties.

[Huxley offered] the idea that modernism itself has some deficiencies or some weaknesses. You get tired of living without a system of values, tired of living on your irony and your wit and you begin to look for something more substantial, more perennial. And this is what turns Huxley towards the East, where he looks at the Eastern mystics and produces novels like *Time Must Have a Stop* and an anthology on mystical writing such as *The Perennial Philosophy.*

Huxley is one of those writers, if you read him and you believe him, you have to change the way you live and the way you look at the world, and that's not necessarily true about Joyce or Virginia Woolf.

For me, Huxley is a "Man for all Seasons." You can read him when you are young and irreverent and as you get older and maybe look for more positive answers, he'll be there to give you some clues as well.

The clues pertain to reconsideration. Maybe to being quieter, getting out of your own way, sitting still, thinking more, looking inside yourself, listening to see if there is anything that's trying to get in touch with you. A voice from beyond or from within; and possibly maybe they are one and the same.

Pierre Vitoux

[Why do we need Huxley today?] I think we've needed Huxley for quite a long time. If I think back on the way he is known in France, *Point Counter Point* and *Brave New World* were read by the French public because they were fairly popular and translated immediately. Huxley is someone who everybody knows and has at least read one or two books. After the war, there was always this extremely intriguing and challenging conversion of Huxley to different attitudes, different values, which is something we haven't done exploring now.

Bernfried Nugel

Even if you don't get easy solutions, or easy results, you shouldn't forget man is a being that can strive for more, not only experience but also knowledge and understanding; and that's the basic legacy on Huxley's part to his readers. If they see that he is still on his way, that he is in the process of trying to arrive somewhere, not having to arrive. That's the general misconception: people think, well, Huxley is the arrogant polymath who preaches and prescribes the rules for a future society.

No, on the contrary, he is the man who is on his way. He is in the process of enlarging his own knowledge and the knowledge of his readers and not only knowledge in the sense of a system of facts or a system of learning, but also in the sense of understanding. I mean "direct experience": this was his magic word in his later works, he was much more interested in direct experience, in transcendental spheres of human life.

NOTES

(Introduction)

1. *Writers at Work: The Paris Review Interviews,* 2nd series, ed. Malcolm Cowley (New York: Viking, 1963), p. 204.

2. Richard Chase, "Yogi-Bogey," *Partisan Review* (May 1942), p. 262.

3. Jerome Meckier, "Housebreaking Huxley: Saint Versus Satirist," *Mosaic,* vol. 5, no. 3, 1972, pp. 166–177. Huxley's religious studies in World War II resulted in the *Perennial Philosophy* (New York: Harper & Row, 1944) and the overlooked essay "Introduction," in Prabhavananda and Isherwood, translators, *The Song of God: Bhagavad-Gita* (New York: Mentor/New American Library, 1944).

4. Eben Bass, *Aldous Huxley, An Annotated Bibliography of Criticism* (New York: Garland, 1981), p. xi.

5. For a complete listing of recorded interviews in this project, see David Dunaway, *Huxley in Hollywood* (New York: Harper, 1989/ London: Bloomsbury, 1989/New York: Anchor Books, 1990), pp. 439–440. Matthew Huxley (Aldous and Maria's only child) and his children have sealed their entire transcripts.

6. Barry Gifford and Larry Lee, *Jack's Box: An Oral Biography* (New York: St. Martin's Press, 1978); Peter Manso, *Mailer* (New York: Simon & Schuster, 1985).

7. This symposium is reprinted in *Aldous Huxley: A Collection of Critical Essays,* Robert Kuehn, ed. (Englewood Cliffs, N.J.: Prentice-Hall, 1985).

(Chapter I)

1. For further biographical details, see Sybille Bedford, *Aldous Huxley* (New York: Knopf/Harper & Row, 1973, 1974) and Grover Smith, ed., *Letters of Aldous Huxley* (New York: Harper & Row, 1968). Note that Smith published only one-quarter of those letters he located.

2. Jocelyn Brooke, *Aldous Huxley* (London: Longmans, 1954). In particular, see John Atkins, *Aldous Huxley* (London: Orion, 1953, 1968), Phillip Thody, *Aldous Huxley: A Biographical Introduction* (New York: Routledge & Kegan Paul, 1975).

3. F. Scott Fitzgerald, writing in the *St. Paul Daily News*, Feb. 26, 1922, cited in Donald Watt, *Aldous Huxley: The Critical Heritage* (London: Routledge & Kegan Paul, 1975).

4. For British and American publication dates of Huxley's books, see the bibliography in *Huxley in Hollywood* (New York: Harper & Row/Bessie Books, London: Bloomsbury, 1989), pp. 442–445.

5. Jocelyn Brooke, *Aldous Huxley* (London: Longmans, 1954), p. 9.

6. Stephen Spender, *Letters to Christopher,* Lee Bartlett, ed. (Santa Barbara, Calif.: Black Sparrow Press, 1980), p. 120. Stephen Spender, "Open Letter to Aldous Huxley," *Left Review* (June 1936).

7. Julian Huxley, *Memories* (New York: Harper & Row, 1970), p. 20.

8. Julian Huxley, *Memories* (New York: Harper & Row, 1970), p. 20.

9. Juliette Huxley, *Leaves of the Tulip Tree* (Topsfield, Mass.: Salem House Publishers, 1986), pp. 189–190.

10. Sandra Darroch, *Ottoline: The Life of Lady Ottoline Morrell* (New York: Coward, McCann, 1975), p. 191.

11. Matthew Huxley was interviewed by the author in March and June 1985 and in August 1988.

12. Juliette Huxley, *Leaves of the Tulip Tree* (Topsfield, Mass.: Salem House Publishers, 1986), pp. 54–55.

13. This episode is quoted in Bedford, pp. 80–81.

14. Quoted in S. P. Rosenbaum, *The Bloomsbury Group* (Toronto: University of Toronto Press, 1975), p. 22.

15. David Bradshaw, *The Hidden Huxley* (London: Faber, 1994).

16. Among the works of Gerald Heard that influenced Huxley are *Science in the Making* (London: Faber, 1935); *The Source of Civilization* (New York: Harper & Brothers, 1937); and his later work, such as *Training for the Life of the Spirit* (New York: Steiner Books, 1957). In particular, Heard's wartime fiction paralleled Huxley's own; for a discussion, see David Dunaway, "Literary Correspondence: Huxley and Heard," *Aldous Huxley Symposium Volume*, with Bernfried Nugel, ed. (Berlin: Peter Verlag, 1995).

17. Note that earlier, Naomi Mitchison refers to the same incident as drawn from her son's experience.

(Chapter II)

1. Grover Smith, *The Letters of Aldous Huxley* (New York: Harper & Row, 1968), pp. 473–474.

2. Interview with Matthew Huxley, June 11, 1985.

3. The majority of these attacks occurred in the pages of the *Left Review* in 1936; in particular see "An Open Letter to Aldous Huxley" in June of that year, and a pamphlet by C. Day Lewis, "We're Not Going to Do Nothing," published by the *Left Review Press*.

4. For an excellent discussion of Aldous Huxley's film career, see Virginia Clark, *Aldous Huxley and Film* (Metuchen, N.J.: Scarecrow Press, 1987).

5. The Hubble Collection at the Huntington Library details social gatherings with the Huxleys from 1937 to 1954.

6. For details on the Loss-Huxley friendship, see "MGM Makes Room for a Genius," in Anita Loos, *Fate Keeps on Happening* (New York: Dodd, Mead, 1984), pp. 166–173.

7. Note that though Lawrence Powell characterizes Huxley as a writer, rather than a scholar, Powell regularly used the UCLA library facilities to furnish Huxley with sources in three languages for Huxley's research—including a number in sixteenth-century French and Latin, for *Grey Eminence.*

8. Interview with the author, March 17, 1985.

9. This letter, dated November 19, 1938, is reprinted in Grover Smith, *Letters of Aldous Huxley* (New York: Harper & Row, 1969), p. 439.

(Chapter III)

1. Aldous Huxley, *The Perennial Philosophy* (New York: Harper & Row, 1944), p. 79.

2. Documents released to the author under the Freedom of Information Act from the Federal Bureau of Information and the U.S. Immigration and Naturalization Service, 1987–1988. At one point the F.B.I. sent an underlined copy of *Brave New World* to Washington for cryptical analysis. The F.B.I. released to the author approximately 150 pages of materials on Huxley. The majority of files concern his later years, when the F.B.I. classified him as marginally subversive (for broadcasting on the maverick, left-wing radio station in L.A., KPFK-FM). Yet the files begin on his arrival in the United States and include references to World War II (when Huxley's pacifism was suspect). In addition, the author obtained District files of the Immigration and Naturalization Service in Los Angeles; this material contains exact dates of Huxley's entries into the United States, as well as materials on his naturalization application.

3. David Dunaway, "Literary Correspondences: Aldous Huxley and Gerald Heard," in *Aldous Huxley Centennial Symposium* (Munich: Peter Verlag, 1995). Grace Hubble, in her diaries in the Huntington Library, mentions on December 3, 1939, that Gerald was no longer quoting Huxley or their letters.

(Chapter IV)

1. [To be determined]

2. Aldous Huxley, *The Devils of Loudon* (New York: Harper & Brothers, 1952), p. 220.

3. This story is corroborated by an article in the *Saturday Review*, April 12, 1952, p. 3.

4. [To be determined]

5. See T. H. Huxley's comments on spiritualism in Leonard Huxley's *Life and Letters*, and in Jeffrey Michlove's *The Roots of Consciousness* (New York: Random House, 1975), pp. 95–98.

6. Interview with Sylvia Nys O'Neill, Aldous Huxley's niece, June 21, 1985.

7. In his published letters, Huxley states clearly that he always intended the work to refer to D. H. and Frieda Lawrence; see Smith, pp. 830–831.

(Chapter V)

1. Professor Bernfried Nugel of the University of Münster is reconstructing the original text of *Island*, before cuts suggested by Harper and by Chatto, Huxley's publishers. The principal collections of correspondence relating to this episode can be found in the Harper & Row Collection at UCLA's Special Collections Library.

2. An essay on Huxley by Guin Nance (*Virginia Quarterly Review*, Winter 1990) suggests that his experiences of transcendence may be the central question for biographers of Huxley.

3. *Island* (New York: Harper & Brothers, 1961), p. 284.

4. Laura Huxley, *This Timeless Moment* (New York: Farrar, Strauss, & Giroux, 1968).

5. Christopher Isherwood, *My Guru and His Disciple* (New York: Farrar, Strauss, & Giroux, 1980), p. 259.

(Chapter VI)

1. Julian Huxley, *Aldous Huxley* (New York: Harper & Row, 1965).

2. Robert Kuehn, *Aldous Huxley: A Collection of Critical Essays* (Englewood Cliffs, N.J.: Prentice-Hall, 1974).

Acknowledgments

A book based on oral sources should reserve its greatest thanks for those whose words made the work possible: the contributors who gave their time to document and memorialize Aldous Huxley. Thanks for your time; thanks for the memories.

Many fine transcribers assisted me: Lisa Hilber, Rebecca Zerger, Becky Chisman; Juliette Cunico, Ph.D., was the most consistently involved. Additional assistants helped in the final stages, particularly Sara Ranney.

Around most major cultural figures, an enterprising empire surfaces; I have found considerable differences in the way such establishments view the critics and historians who approach them. In the case of Huxley, those involved seem to be motivated by illumination and grace, as Aldous was.

I owe a debt of thanks to the various members of the Huxley family, particularly Laura Huxley and her agent Dorris Halsey, for assistance and encouragement.

To the Huntington Library in San Marino, California, where the original transcripts of these interviews are filed, I am grateful. May their materials on Aldous Huxley make them a leading center for Huxley studies in the twenty-first century. Let me also thank the Huxley scholars who contributed to the last chapter: Peter Firchow, Kirpal Singh, Guin Nance, Jerome Meckier, James Sexton, Philip Thody, Pierre Vitoux, and Bernfield Nugel.

My agent, Loretta Barrett, and my editor, Kent Carroll, have sustained me by their enthusiasm for Huxley and for this book. Similarly, I thank the Wallerstein family, Lillian and Bob Ross, Nina Wallerstein, and particularly Alexander Wallerstein Dunaway for being patient.

Lastly, to Aldous Huxley I must pass my thanks for giving me the opportunity to know more of his world and to share it with the many others who now more than ever turn to his works to find inspiration and hints of salvation for a troubled world. Huxley, like Thomas More, is a man for all seasons, and some of these have yet to dawn.

CHECKLIST OF MAJOR PUBLICATIONS AND RESIDENCES

(This listing is intended as a reader's guide to this volume, rather than to replace the extensive chronologies of Huxley's life in the authorized, two-volume biography, *Aldous Huxley* (New York: Knopf/Harper & Row, 1973, 1974) by Sybil Bedford and the collected correspondence, *Letters of Aldous Huxley* (New York: Harper & Row, 1969), edited by Grover Smith. For publication dates of the British and American editions of Huxley's books, see David Dunaway, *Huxley in Hollywood* (New York: Bessie Books/Harper & Row, 1989; London: Bloomsbury, 1989; New York: Anchor, 1990, pp. 442–445.

1894 Aldous Leonard Huxley born in Surrey, England, July 26.

1903 H. attends preparatory school at Hillside.

1908 H. enrolls at Eton; his mother, Julia Arnold, dies suddenly.

1911 H. blinded by keratitis; learns braille, visits Naomi Mitchison Haldane in Oxford.

1913 H. begins Balliol College (Oxford), visits Ottoline Morrell's house, Garsington.

1914 Death of Trevenen Huxley, 24, H.'s older brother.

1915 H.'s first published poem, in Oxford Poetry of 1915.

1917 H. meets Bloomsbury circle in London, teaches at Eton.

1919 H. moves to Hampstead, London; marries Maria Nys, becomes staff writer for The Athenaeum.

1920 H. publishes first book of stories, *Limbo,* and a third collection of verse, *Leda.*

175

1921 H. acquires agent, publishes first novel, *Crome Yellow.*

1923 H. publishes *Antic Hay,* moves to Florence, Italy.

1925 Publication of *Those Barren Leaves*; H. begins round-the-world trip chronicled in *Jesting Pilate.*

1927 The Huxleys move to Forte de Marmi, Italy; Christmas with D. H. and Frieda Lawrence.

1928 The Huxleys move in with Maria's sister Jeanne outside Paris; *Point Counter Point* is published, becomes best-seller.

1930 H. publishes *Brief Candles;* family moves to Sanary, France.

1931 H. in London for production of a play, *The World of Light.*

1932 H. edits *Selected Letters of D. H. Lawrence,* publishes *Brave New World* and *Texts and Pretexts.*

1933 Huxleys travel through Central America, Caribbean, Mexico, United States.

1934 H. encounters writer's block in finishing *Eyeless in Gaza;* he and Maria winter in London.

1935 H. cures depression and insomnia, becomes active pacifist, begins physical reeducation lessons, meditation.

1936 *Eyeless in Gaza, The Olive Tree* published.

1937 The Huxley family and Gerald Heard move to United States, drive to Lawrence ranch in New Mexico; *Ends and Means* published.

1938 Huxley and Heard finish lecture tour on pacifism; Huxleys stay in Hollywood and Beverly Hills; H. receives first film-writing contract from MGM studios.

1939 H. moves to Pacific Palisades, north of Santa Monica Canyon in Los Angeles; publishes first fiction written in United States, *After Many a Summer.*

1941 Publication of Huxley's first biography, *Grey Eminence;* family moves out of Los Angeles to Llano in Mojave Desert following Pearl Harbor.

1942 H. works on film script of *Jane Eyre,* publishes *Art of Seeing.*

1944 Huxleys live in Llano, with apartment in Beverly Hills; *Time Must Have a Stop* published.

1945 H. falls ill at Llano, publishes *The Perennial Philosophy.*

1946 *Science, Liberty and Peace* published; H. works on screenplay for *The Gioconda Smile*, the first film made of his writing; the Huxleys prepare to leave Llano.

1948 Huxley family moves to Wrightwood, Calif., then visits Europe; *Ape and Essence* is published.

1949 Huxleys buy house on North King's Road, at the edge of Hollywood.

1950 Huxleys visit England and Europe; H.'s play *The Gioconda Smile* opens on Broadway; *Themes and Variations* is published.

1951 H. blinded for a second time, following a case of iritis.

1952 *Devils of Loudun* published; Maria Huxley operated on for breast cancer; the disease reoccurs in six months.

1953 H. experiments with mescaline at King's Road house.

1954 *Doors of Perception* is published; Huxleys visit Europe and Middle East.

1955 Maria Huxley dies; H. publishes *The Genius and the Goddess;* summers in Connecticut, then returns to Los Angeles.

1956 H. marries Laura Archera and moves to Hollywood Hills, on Deronda Drive; *Heaven and Hell, Tomorrow and Tomorrow and Tomorrow* are published.

1958 Huxleys visit Brazil, England, France, Italy.

1960 H. lectures at University of California, Berkeley, The Menninger Foundation, M.I.T.; his cancer of the tongue is diagnosed.

1961 Huxley's Hollywood residence burns; Huxleys move to Mulholland Drive, Hollywood.

1962 *Island* published; H. lectures in Berkeley, Santa Barbara, New Mexico, New York, Brussels.

1963 Huxley dies in Los Angeles, November 22, 1963.

CONTRIBUTORS

Don Bachardy

Mr. Bachardy, the well-known portraitist, was born in 1934 and grew up in Los Angeles, near Glendale. On a Santa Monica beach at the mouth of the canyon, he met Christopher Isherwood, and through him, Aldous and Maria Huxley in 1953. Educated in an art school in L.A., Bachardy became prominent in southern California's arts and literary community. From the mid-1950s on, he and Isherwood met Aldous and Maria Huxley at dinner parties and social occasions. The interview took place in 1989, a year after the death of Isherwood, in the house in which they lived together for decades.

Abigail Bok

Ms. Bok was born in Los Angeles in 1955, growing up in Malibu and then Beverly Hills. After graduating from Princeton, she worked as a book editor, alternating between Los Angeles and the East Coast. For the last dozen years, she has worked as an editor for New York publishers and as a research fellow at UCLA. Our interview took place in 1989, in her home near Los Angeles. The granddaughter of Peggy Kiskadden, her childhood memories of Aldous Huxley are of his last years.

Sidney Field

The late Sidney Field was born in Puerto Rico, from which he emigrated to the United States in the mid-1920s. His family were founders of the Theosophical Society, and he soon met Jiddu Krishnamurti. Field attended Hollywood High School and the University of California at Los Angeles. He met Aldous and Maria Huxley at the Happy Valley School in the 1950s, when Aldous was on its board of directors. By virtue of his studies of the Theosophical Society and his firsthand acquaintance of Krishnamurti, Huxley's friend and spiritual colleague, Field in 1985 traced the important relationship between these two figures.

Dorris Halsey

Dorris Halsey was the French-born wife of Reese Halsey, an English professor who became Huxley's agent at the William Morris Agency, representing him in many of his film-related projects during the 1940s and '50s. After her husband's death, Dorris Halsey continues to represent the Huxley estate as a longtime friend and associate of Mrs. Laura Huxley. She was interviewed in her house in Los Angeles on August 12, 1985.

Ellen Hovde

Ms. Hovde grew up in Pittsburgh, Pennsylvania, the daughter of a professor and public administrator. She attended the Carnegie Mellon Institute, majoring in theater. After a stay in Norway, she returned to New York where, in 1949, she met and married Matthew Huxley, Aldous and Maria's only child, when he was working at the Elmer Roper polling agency. They had two children, Trevenen and Tessa Huxley. In 1955, after Maria Huxley's death, Aldous spent the summer with Ellen and Matthew Huxley in Connecticut; Aldous remained close to Hovde until his death.

Today Hovde is a prominent film director, and the interview took place in the office of her film production company in New York, on March 20, 1986.

Francis Huxley

Francis Huxley, the youngest son of Julian Huxley, Aldous's brother, was born in England in 1923. After service in the Royal Navy he entered Balliol College, Oxford, where he studied zoology. A taste for travel led him to zoological fieldwork in Gambia and anthropological fieldwork in the Amazon basin of Brazil. Eventually he moved to the United States and continued research into the social anthropology of a Canadian mental hospital and traveled to Haiti to study voodoo. Author of a range of books on the anthropology of consciousness, Francis Huxley was interviewed in his flat in London on July 10, 1985. His preface to this volume was written in 1990. He lives today in New Mexico.

Lady Juliette Huxley

Lady Huxley was born Juliette Baillot in Switzerland in 1896; after her education she came to England as a governess for the daughter of Sir Phillip and Lady Ottoline Morrell. The Morrells hosted Britain's between-wars intelligentsia; among the many important friends and influences whom Juliette (and Aldous Huxley) met at their home were Bertrand Russell, Lytton Strachey, and Katherine Mansfield. There Juliette met Julian Huxley, whom she married in March 1919, five months before Aldous married Maria Nys.

Over the next four decades, Juliette Huxley was a frequent hostess to Aldous and Maria Huxley during their sporadic visits to England. (Recollections of these visits are included in her memoir, *Leaves of the Tulip Tree*.) The late Mrs. Huxley lived in the house she shared with her husband of over fifty years. The interview was conducted on July 5, 1985, in her library, overlooking a now-busy street in the Belsize Park district of London.

Laura Archera Huxley

Mrs. Huxley was born in the first decade of the century near Turino, Italy, to well-to-do parents who raised her to be a concert violinist. Arriving in New York to study music in the late 1930s, she was marooned in America by World War II. Eventually she moved to California, where she worked as a violinist and then a film editor. She met Aldous and Maria Huxley in the late 1940s and saw them socially until Maria Huxley's death in 1955. Laura and Aldous were married just over a year later. The couple's home in the Hollywood Hills was burned down when a fire wiped out their possessions in 1961, after which they both moved in with Laura's longtime friend, Ms. Virginia Pfeiffer, until Aldous Huxley's death from cancer in 1963. Subsequently, Ms. Huxley continued her career as a therapist and author. Her works include *You Are Not the Target; The Child of Your Dreams; OneADayReason to be Happy;* and her memoir of Aldous Huxley, *This Timeless Moment.* Her recollections were made in the summer of 1985.

Christopher Isherwood

Mr. Isherwood was born in Cheshire, England, in 1904 to a wealthy family. He left Cambridge without graduating and became a published author at twenty-four. He traveled with W. H. Auden in China, pre-war Berlin, and New York, before moving to Hollywood "to clarify my ideas about pacifism by talking to Gerald Heard and Aldous Huxley." Heard, Huxley, and Isherwood were all ardent students of Hinduism. In L.A., Isherwood wrote films, memoirs, and plays, collaborating on a half-dozen projects with Aldous Huxley, whom he also saw socially, often in the company of his companion, Don Bachardy.

Margaret (Peggy) Kiskadden

Ms. Kiskadden was born in the suburbs of Philadelphia in 1904 and lived there until she married the writer Curtis Bok. Subsequently she lived in Santa Fe and England before settling in Beverly Hills. Through mutual friends, she had met the Huxleys before their emigration and subsequently greeted them on their arrival in California in 1937. For the next twenty-five years she was an intimate friend of Aldous and Maria. Her sons, Benjamin and Derek Bok (lately president of Harvard University), were friends of Matthew Huxley, while her second husband, the Los Angeles surgeon Bill Kiskadden, served as Huxley's principal medical adviser. The interviews with Ms. Kiskadden took place in her home in Beverly Hills in the summers of 1985 and 1988.

Mary Anita Loos

Like her aunt, Anita Loos, Ms. Mary Anita Loos was born in San Diego, but moved to the Los Angeles area as a teenager, where the family lived approximately a mile away from Anita Loos's mansion on what is today the Pacific Coast Highway. Anita Loos was one of the first professional screenwriters in the United States, and her circle of acquaintances (including Louis B. Mayer, Charlie Chaplin, and Darryl Zanuck) was the world in which Mary Anita was raised. She met Aldous and Maria at one of the Sunday brunches her aunt gave for Hollywood's literati. Mary Anita Loos went on to a career as a novelist and screenwriter. As a relative of perhaps Aldous and Maria's closest friend, Mary Anita visited the Huxley homes and for decades remained close to the family.

Burgess Meredith

Mr. Meredith, a leading stage actor in the 1930s whose half-century career in film included some forty films, was born in 1908. Probably best known today for his television work (particularly in the series *Batman*), his acting in such films as *Of Mice and Men* and *Day of the Locust* brought him widespread international recognition. He met Huxley in the late Forties, after co-acting with (and marrying) Paulette Goddard. In the period his reminiscences cover, from 1946 to 1949, Meredith and Goddard hoped to film Huxley's classic novel *Brave New World* and became early witnesses to Huxley's experiments with hypnosis and parapsychology. The interview took place in the actor's studio-residence in Malibu in August 1986.

Lady Naomi [Haldane] Mitchison

Ms. Naomi Mitchison, author of two dozen books, was a longtime family friend of Aldous Huxley; she was the daughter of Professor John Scott Haldane of Oxford and sister of J. B. S. Haldane, the biologist. Mitchison was particularly close to Aldous during the years of his teenage blindness, and in his first days at Oxford, where she was also friends with his brother Trev and with Lewis Gielgud, brother of the now-famous actor Sir John Gielgud. As one of the few living childhood friends of Aldous Huxley, her reminiscences are an invaluable source for the author's younger years. This interview took place over a two-day period by telephone from London to her family's estate in Scotland on June 18–19, 1990.

Jeanne Nys Moulaert Neveux

Ms. Neveux, a younger sister of Maria Huxley, was born in Belgium and, like the rest of her siblings, was a war refugee moving from Scotland to Italy to Paris, where she arrived in the early 1920s as the wife of a theater designer. Despite repeated urgings from the Huxleys to emigrate to the United States, Ms. Neveux lived in Europe almost all her life. For decades she worked as a therapist, practicing the method of visual training developed by Dr. W. H. Bates. Ms. Neveux was interviewed in her Paris flat in July 1985.

Lawrence Powell

Dr. Lawrence Powell, one of California's foremost academic librarians, was born in Washington, D.C., but grew up in southern California. He took his doctorate in France and, soon after his return to California, worked for Jacob Zeitlin, the distinguished bookseller. It was at Zeitlin's shop that he first met Aldous Huxley. In subsequent years he worked at UCLA's library, where he helped Huxley obtain the rare and obscure books needed for the author's research. Dean Powell was interviewed in his office at the University of Arizona in Tucson on December 10, 1985.

Rosalind Rajagopal

Ms. Rajagopal was born in Buffalo, New York, moving to California when she was sixteen, in 1919. Her older sister was a Theosophist who ran a school for devotees. In 1922, she met the Theosophist spiritual leader, Jiddu Krishnamurti, and his brother. Some fifteen years later, when Aldous and Maria moved to California, a mutual friend suggested the Huxleys meet Rosalind Rajagopal, beginning a friendship that lasted until the end of the Huxleys' lives. For decades she was the director of the Happy Valley School in Ojai, with which Krishnamurti and Huxley were both associated. The interview took place in her house at Ojai in the summer of 1985.

Betty (Beth) Wendel

Ms. Wendel was born in San Francisco in 1902, moving to the Los Angeles area in 1933 with her husband, Sanford Wendel. She began her career as a writer, contributing pieces to *The New Yorker* long before meeting Aldous Huxley. Her subsequent career as a Hollywood script doctor brought her into the circle of Anita Loos, and it was at one of Loos's Sunday gatherings that she met Aldous and Maria Huxley. Subsequently she was a colleague and a friend to the Huxleys, working for several years with Aldous on the dramatization of his writing—in particular the financially unsuccessful Broadway adaptation of *The Genius and The Goddess*. She was interviewed in her house near Beverly Hills in June and August 1985.

Rose Nys D'Haulleville Wessberg

The youngest of four daughters of Marguerite Baltus and

Norbert Nys, Ms. Wessberg was born in 1912 in Belgium. Before finishing her schooling, the arrival of the German army drove her sisters—including the eldest, Maria, Aldous Huxley's first wife—to Glasgow, where their uncle was a professor of fine arts.

The family moved to Italy during the war, returning to Britain and to Belgium afterward. In 1935, Rose married the Surrealist poet [Baron] Eric D'Haulleville. They had one daughter, Olivia, before her husband died; Rose subsequently remarried an American diplomat, William Wessberg, and emigrated to the United States in 1942. Aldous and Maria bought a house for her and her new baby Sigfrid near their wartime home in Llano, California.

Ms. Nys was interviewed in a convalescent home near Palmdale, on the western edge of California's Mojave Desert, in August 1985.

Sigfrid Wessberg

Mr. Sigfrid Wessberg was the nephew by marriage of Aldous Huxley; his mother was Rose Nys, Maria's youngest sister. Siggy grew up in California in the 1950s, often visiting the Huxleys at their home in Llano. He attended Happy Valley School, under the directorship of Rosalind Rajagopal, and in later years he visited the Huxleys at their house in Hollywood; he remembers these visits from the standpoint of a member of a younger generation. The interview took place in his house in Burbank in February 1988.

Jacob Zeitlin

Mr. Zeitlin was born in Racine, Wisconsin, in 1902 to a Russian Jewish immigrant family. Jake, as he came to be known, grew up in Fort Worth, Texas, where he won the Texas State Poetry Award in 1922. In 1925, he arrived in Los Angeles, where he worked as a journalist and eventually founded Zeitlin and Ver Brugge, one of America's most successful rare book stores. Zeitlin represented writers such as D. H. Lawrence and Aldous Huxley on film projects in Hollywood; he was one of the first to greet the Huxleys on their arrival in California. For more than twenty-five years, Zeitlin obtained rare books for Huxley's research and became one of his close friends in Los Angeles. The interview took place in Zeitlin's home, near his famous Red Barn Bookshop on La Cienega Boulevard in Los Angeles in 1985. As the second interview took place, Zeitlin's health was already in decline, prior to his death in 1987.

THE ALDOUS HUXLEY
ORAL HISTORY PROJECT

Nearly one hundred interviews, a third of them tape-recorded, were conducted in England, in France, and in the United States (from New Hampshire to southern California), over a four-year period from 1985 to 1989.

As with all field research, the responses varied considerably. Some interviewees were more candid than others; others more anxious to seal evidence and anecdotes in history's deep freeze. Some used their interviews to bludgeon enemies; others, to right old wrongs or to shape up their position in the historical record. Excepting Greta Garbo, no one refused my request for an interview. (Additional information about the interviewees in this volume is found in the section "Contributors.") This note is offered to the reader as an explanation of my method and approach.

Selection of narrators for an oral history project is a tricky process: one seeks out the "best" narrators, the most eloquent and concise; at the same time, one strives for representativeness. Chosen for this volume were those with firsthand observations of Aldous Huxley, particularly family members, friends, and colleagues; eighty percent of the contributors fall into these three categories. Yet those with smaller roles in Huxley's life—ranging from his cook to his librarian—were also included. (As mentioned in the Introduction, a dearth of narrators surviving from Huxley's earliest years skewed available oral testimony slightly toward Huxley's American period.)

Huxley's circle was a select one, including a number of internationally known actors, authors, and filmmakers. They are articulate, yet mindful of how remarks could be misconstrued out of context or sensationalized. A few narrators— approximately one out of twenty—sealed passages of their interviews, though such restrictions include, at most, four percent of their transcript. (In no instance did I seal comments in a transcript unilaterally.)

The interviews of course varied in their formality and circumstances; specific interview histories for each session are included with the original transcripts at the Huntington Library in San Marino, California. These histories describe the physical settings, moods, and other dynamics of the interviews, which are open to scholarly research.

Of the approximately two thousand pages of transcript generated by the project, only a fraction could be printed here. Criteria for inclusion were passages I found informative, thoughtful, and those (few) bearing directly on his literary process. If Huxley had any literary confidants, they are apparently deceased for some years. (The Grace Hubble Collection at the Huntington Library contains literary insights; she periodically worked as Huxley's proofreader.)

Questions asked of narrators were roughly similar and parallel. Oral history provides an excellent example of the circular, formative-evaluation process of qualitative research: the inquiry is refined subtly after each new bit of information is recorded. Though the overall directions of the inquiry do not change, for a given interview specific questions will. The core question areas were Huxley's work in literature and films; his aesthetic and political priorities; his life with friends and family; his exploration of alternative ways of seeing and mysticism; and the subculture of Hollywood in which he found himself.

Descriptions of oral history projects customarily include mention of the interviewer/researcher. Some of this personal background can be gleaned from the prologue to *Huxley in Hollywood,* particularly my motivation for writing that book, my early experiences reading Huxley, and that of a generation that discovered his works in the 1960s. My background includes training in literary and historical research at the University of California, Berkeley, and a rather bohemian upbringing in Greenwich Village. My parents read and appreciated iconoclasts such as Huxley.

I conducted all the interviews with individuals whom I initially knew only as names. My direct preparation was reading previous biographical and critical works, enhanced as the project proceeded by new understandings from new interviews.

My role was one of encouraging historical testimony, discouraging nothing yet directing the session's course toward questions previously identified as crucial to situating the writer's life and work in a larger context of Anglo-American literary history. This objective led to interviews distinctly different from those designed for broadcast or daily journalism, which tend to focus on eliciting emotion and sensation.

Oral historians are both history's advocates and their narrators' collaborators. Sometimes we urge a narrator onward in service of the first goal, even against the possibility of disturbing the second. Two masters, as Jesus remarked in the New Testament, require different attentions: ''Render unto Caesar, what is Caesar's.'' At the cutting edge of oral historical inquiry, questions are asked that may be uncomfortable to answer, or even to contemplate.

Previously published oral history anthologies have assisted as models for the present work.[1] Arrangers of a book of this sort make structural-historical decisions crucial to the work's readership and use. Should interviews be arranged by narrator or by topic? In chronological or topical order? In a call-and-response pattern, which juxtaposes differing accounts, or in a holistic fashion, which deemphasizes differing viewpoints?

I lean toward the juxtaposition mode and have offered, for example, sharply diverse accounts of the effect on Huxley of the fire that destroyed his library and possessions and of the effect of Huxley's eye exercises. (This strategy might be contrasted with that of Studs Terkel, who weaves his interviews seamlessly, with few contradictions, which partly explains why his books are so readable.)

The fusion of written sources and interviews has been called "oral biography," a genre that may possess advantages over works limited to written sources: interview sessions expose new collections of documents, including letters and photographs; interviews cover a full range of the subject's life, not just periods of public activity; the sources themselves are available for cross-examination and correction of the record; and, finally, orally sourced biography has an authenticity based on the triangular collaboration among the biographer, the sources, and occasionally, though not in this instance, the subject.

The problems of using interviews as a historical source transcend the homily that just telling something aloud does not make it true. But the "halo effect," as sociologists call the desire of narrators to meet the expectations of interviewers, and the role of verbal performance must be factored into any assessment of oral sources.

Oral accounts mediate between previous life events and an interviewer's contemporary, research-based frame of reference. Because collecting oral sources for biographical research involves eliciting narration, aesthetic formulae, and discourse, rules of storytelling skew the information received in sometimes subtle ways. The narrator configures actual events into a symbolic representation of personal mythology, often based on hindsight and readings of subsequently written history. Factors affecting oral performance of personalized historical narratives—audiences' historical and immediate self-justification and catharsis, to name but a few—cannot be ignored. Many interviews inevitably yield "set pieces," rehearsed anecdotes of the past that are more prone to story than to history. Often one must collect such anecdotes that our narrators are so eager to deliver before one can formulate the facts of a historical situation. Such well-worn stories often come to have a life of their own.

(I remember spending three months narrowing down a key date in the life of Pete Seeger—when he first heard the five-string banjo that became his musical trademark. After writing the North Carolina State Library for a list of performers at a festival on two separate years and reinterviewing his father [who took him there], I came up with a date that contradicted every printed source. When I broached my evidence, Pete Seeger agreed and lamented that for thirty years he had been giving out an erroneous one. The following week I heard him tell an interviewer from National Public Radio the original, incorrect date.)

Clearly there is no royal road to historically objective truth, in oral history or any other variety. Indeed, so many post-modernist theorists challenge the notion that "facts" exist at all that we can barely be sure that the twelfth century existed or that a man called Christopher Columbus actually landed in the Caribbean. Huxley would have found such quandaries amusing yet perhaps uninformative. At the end of the day, as Pascal warned us, all we have go on is faith: that a man lived and wrote and that a few still recollect him and his work.

TRANSCRIBING AND EDITING ORAL HISTORY

Transcribing Oral History

Oral history is by no means an uncomplicated process; a general discussion of transcribing and editing oral history is in order.

Just as no tape recording can duplicate the multilayered complexity of the interview, so no transcript, either in raw or edited form, can convey the entire significance of the tape. Researchers analyzing interviews often focus on sociolinguistic features, to study conversational analysis, body language, and other interactions between narrator and interviewer (including pauses or untranscribable features that indicate emphasis, reaction, or uncertainty).

To translate oral discourse into written form involves the elimination of direct repetitions (such as an anecdote or a phrase) and open and closing formulae ("Yes" or "Well"); substituting names for indefinite pronouns; the addition of punctuation; rearrangement of paragraphs to eliminate digressions and, in a few cases, by embedding my questions in brackets. These are edited and excerpted transcripts; if left in question-and-answer format, the testimony would have doubled in length and been more tiresome to read. Scholars with a particular need to study the interviews are invited to do so at the Huntington Library. Such editing procedures are standard in preparing oral history transcripts for public consumption.[1]

The transcribers, postgraduate students in English, assisted me in mediating between oral and written forms of the language: verbatim transcripts are tiresome to read, containing every false start, rephrasing, and recursive meandering. Additional editing entailed collapsing stories originally told in multiple parts into single versions and conjoining comments on parallel topics. Principal transcribers for this collection were Lisa Hilber, Rebecca Zerger, Rebecca Chisman, and Juliette Cunico.

Transcription, the rendering of a printed record from a field recording, is necessarily imperfect. Oral language relies on inflection, pacing, emotional color, tonal intonations, and other devices, but these are not easily rendered on a printed page. Nor are body language or sociolinguistic features (such as eye contact, physical proximity, gesture) visible to the readers of transcripts. Such details may be found in a history of a particular interview, alongside the context of the performance or collection: its location, date, participants, and other clues to the function of the text. (In the case of the Aldous Huxley Oral History Project, these interview histories are available alongside the transcripts at the Huntington Library in California.)

Behind most practical daily tasks—and transcribing tapes is certainly one of these—lies a superstructure of assumptions. What are these givens for transcribing oral history? What do we find in an oral history transcript?

Oral texts are represented graphically either by transcribing the notes and intervals of a piece of music or by representing what is spoken as a series of words, sentences, and paragraphs on a page. Different methods of transcription are used, as appropriate. At one extreme is the verbatim transcription, a theoretically exact representation of sounds, down to the morphemes and phonemes that compose the language of the performance. Verbatim transcriptions themselves vary. A linguist may include tones and phonetic representation; a sociolinguist might reproduce the pause behavior in a critical utterance; a historian might include a faulty recounting of events alongside a factual one in order to show flaws in the narrator's recollection.

At the other extreme is the interview catalog of topics covered on a tape, broken down into measurable units, such as five-minute segments or tape-counter digital numbers. This postpones the costly and labor-intensive transcription process by providing a general overview of what was collected. Between these two poles are several options: the nonverbatim transcript (in a work such as this one, this means a transcript without the "ums" and false starts); the partial transcription of relevant quotes, and the selective paraphrase. (In this volume, I have edited and excerpted from a verbatim transcript.)

Transcription is an art, not a science, demanding skilled guesses at words and intended meaning. A dilemma lies in preparing a written document for multiple future uses, for some of these (a radio documentary, a legal proceeding) were unascertainable at the time of transcription.

Many oral historians and ethnographers spend their days collecting and processing oral interviews, but few have time to speculate on what users encounter when they sit down to make sense of the transcripts. Beyond the historical content of a transcript, users find a nonwritten tradition, recorded in a unique performance. An interview is but an occasional representation of culture, whether a general's career or a street vendor's life. Because we cannot transcribe an entire culture (or the world view that underlies it), we interview to reassemble or illuminate that tradition. Yet how much can one historical example bring us of the whole, of what anthropologist Clifford Geertz calls the "thickness" of culture?[2] Ultimately, each interview is a tangent to the world it expresses; recollection embodies culture through a combination of traditional formulae and individual memory.

We compensate for the tangential nature of the interview by research and observation, by eliciting information on the interview's context. We design our projects so that the narrators are representative.

A focus on the narrator and his or her historical sources sometimes ignores the symbolic and performance elements of the testimony. Especially after the lifetime of the testimony, many readers may overlook this influence in the transcript.

Willa K. Baum, in the most extended treatment of processing oral history, suggests a central dilemma in transcription. Are we documenting what occurred in the interview?

> At one extreme are those who argue that the tape recording itself is the primary record and that the transcript must mirror that recording as closely as possible. . . . Their goal is to authenticate the interview situation itself, how the narrator and interviewer interacted. . . . There are others who, in the search for historical authenticity, will argue that the transcript is the beginning framework, but that the editor must work with the narrator in checking facts, correcting unclear statements, and adding details. . . .[3]

We should document both ways, Baum concludes, using the interview history for context and the transcript for historical accuracy.

This answer may beg the real question raised: what is being processed, an interview or a series of facts? This distinction becomes sharpest in negotiating contradictions in the record. If the narrator says she recalls her husband having three sons when birth certificates show he fathered four, how do we interpret this discrepancy? That she psychologically dismissed one? That he actually only had three? What we make of this depends, in part, on our purpose: evaluating the memory of the subject or providing data for others. In this work, I in a few instances have presented a best-guess version of what happened, choosing the most creditable account, as corroborated by independent sources. Alternately,

I have included a series of conflicting reports and left the reader to sort out the contradictions.

Resolving this issue is an example of how editorial style reflects deeper judgments. "Do I contradict myself?" Walt Whitman asked in "Leaves of Grass." "Very well then I contradict myself, I am large, I contain multitudes."

Even verbatim transcription (if such a thing is possible) and careful notes cannot re-create the history-telling interview. Adding video recording to audio does not resolve this problem, for it is not words that are told, but an event. No oral history transcript can capture the intimacy that gestures bring, or the smells and snugness of a life recounted in a warm kitchen on a cold day.

The oral interview is a multilayered communicative event, which a transcript only palely reflects. The narrator may have said what we type, but how do we capture those meanings locked out of the transcript in gestures or in emphases through shift in pitch? Some have called for encoding sociolinguistic features in interview transcripts, yet an appropriate system for doing this is still not widely agreed upon.[4] Perhaps the incompleteness of the transcript is not accidental, and the fault lies not in the difficulty of coding sociolinguistic features but in the process of transcription itself.

When we transcribe, we as much re-create as translate. As anyone conversant with more than one language understands instinctively, the special problem of translation is that we often translate words when we mean to translate meanings. Words are only bearers for clusters of cultural associations. To take one classic example, "snow" means one thing to the equatorial African and quite another to the Scandinavian, although each refers to the same physical substance. It is not the snow that differs but its culture-specific associations.

The transcription process may be akin to what Noam Chomsky observed forty years ago about the fundamental structure of language—that the way words come from our mouths is governed by rules we are largely unconscious of, the "deep-structure" as opposed to the "surface-structure" on the edge of our conscious minds.[5] We pause over whether to type "The members who attended were him/he and me/I," even when our narrator's intent is clear. Thus, transcribing requires a sharp and often unconscious application of written grammar to oral presentation, or more formal written expressive rules to casually spoken ones. This is one reason why narrators dislike verbatim transcriptions, which often make them appear illiterate. The divergence between oral and written expression is natural, for in writing we revise and reconsider, but the distinction gives the lie to those claiming transcriptions are absolutely accurate. Accurate to what—to written or oral form? To what was said, or what was recorded? The ethnomusicologist Charles Seeger once compared transcribing music to taking a snapshot of a bird in flight, its motion frozen into a gesture.

From this extreme perspective, transcriptions may be inherently inaccurate. Perhaps the transcription process itself decontextualizes oral information to the point of nonutility. For the transcript is hybrid, neither oral nor written, a shallow reflection of a living, dynamic event. The distance between the transcriber in an office and the interviewer in the field is so great that the distinctions in world view may vanish as the words form into letters on the page. A false sense of participation may be created in the reader of transcripts. Readers might think they receive all the information of the interview; in reality, they are as close as the television viewer who watches a rainforest on the screen and assumes he possesses the experience. In the end, the problems of reading a transcript resemble Plato's famous analogy of the cave dwellers who mistake shadows on the wall for the rich, three-dimensional world of direct experience.

Editing Oral History

Editing may be said to begin with auditing, the process of comparing a transcript to its source recording. Once the transcription is complete in the first draft, the transcriber or interviewer will check it by auditing, which involves the lengthy process of reading the transcript while listening to the tape. Auditing the tape allows the editor to note which spellings, dates, and names need to be verified, and to prepare a basic subject catalog that can be used later for an index and table of contents.

Editing oral texts involves preparing them for future use through arrangement, selection, and annotation. After completing a partial or complete transcription, very often one needs to arrange the stories in a new order or excerpt items for publication or discussion. The editor specifies what has been done to the original recording and, naturally, preserves the tape or transcription in the original form.

Besides rearranging and selecting, editing involves keeping an ear attuned for different details: assuring consistency of names, dates, editorial style, and spelling; noting which stories are segmented (begun and started at different points)— and possibly joining them.

Editing may be the stage of processing where the end product is most directly shaped. In preparing field recordings for use in a museum exhibit or broadcast, editing will involve flagging passages that suit one's purpose and avoiding those that might provoke problems of libel or invasion of privacy. If intended for publication, editing might mean developing criteria for selecting items to be included or developing a typology in which different categories of texts can be distinguished.

Once a recorded text has been transcribed into written form and audited, it requires still another testing: review by the narrator. In oral history, this is done by returning the transcript and having the narrator review it for unintentional errors, such as the classic mistranscription: "They used to have the customers sitting up with the dead." What the narrator actually said was far less macabre: "They used to have the custom of sitting up with the dead."[6] Such errors occasionally slip by the best transcribers and editors. Narrator review also allows the source to add clarifying information or ascertain key dates. This is also the editor's chance to confront contradictions between the existing historical record and the new, oral information. When an informant claims the great flood was in 1922 and published information places the event in 1927, the narrator may not be wrong; perhaps there were two "great floods," and the initial question or answer lacked specificity.

A transcribed oral text is a neutral, seemingly objective (but not uncomplicated) representation of a multidimensional verbal interaction between collector and history-teller. In later uses and analysis, this interaction is colored by the users' subjective visions of what the text represents.[7] The setting of oral texts is their use and analysis, a process illustrated by the six chapters of this work.

Fields relying on oral data share a common ground. We can read an oral narrative from many different angles—literary, historical, anthropological, linguistic—but the text remains the same. Acknowledgment of the cross-fertilization among disciplines—which produces fields such as oral literary history or linguistic anthropology—brings the acuity of multiple perspectives to a common product, the oral text.

ORAL LITERARY HISTORY AND ORAL BIOGRAPHY

Oral Literary History

Oral literary history, the process of documenting via recorded interviews the literary culture of a period, is an ambiguous term referring to the literary side of oral history and to the oral history side of literary history. Oral history can be defined as the tape-recorded recollections of eyewitnesses to historically significant events; oral literary history is the application of the oral history research method to literary topics. Oral biography, such as this work, is one result of such literary study.

A discussion of oral biography entails five parameters from oral literary history. First, oral literary history is applicable primarily to works of contemporary literature, where the researcher interactively probes such elements as the author's intentions, creative process and revisions, critical reception, and networks of influence. Using oral sources to document these topics appears to be relevant only to works created within the past half-century, when living sources are still accessible and memories can be taped.

Second, works studied by oral literary historians tend to be language-centered texts, concerned with what sociolinguists such as John Gumperz and Dell Hymes refer to as "Speech

Acts,'' within the theory of communicative competence.[1] In
the multiplicity of possible narrative stances, the creators (or
tellers) of texts of interest to oral literary historians tend to
be those for whom creation is primarily embedded in verbal
discourse. Oral memoirs of the Vietnam War, which appear
with increasing frequency and reach a wide public audience,
are typical of works narrating a history, event, or person via
eyewitness recollections. The common ground of such texts is
that they are orally generated—spoken, rather than originally
composed in print. Among the advantages of such sources
are their textual information in the way language carries cultural and subcultural signifiers.

Third, texts of interest to oral literary historians contain
explicit historical references that invite elucidation; this is in
contrast to the products of literary movements such as sym-
bolism or post-modernism, where the text is internally refer-
ential and reflexive, to the exclusion of the world outside. By
contrast, an oral literary history of Norman Mailer's novel
Armies of the Night would necessarily use oral sources to re-
create the storming of the Pentagon in 1968, including interviews with Mailer's co-demonstrators, the guards who de-
tained him, and various eyewitnesses. This third factor may
be conceived of as a documentarian's literary history, informed by an ethnographic stance; where cultural and historical patterns are crucial to a work's significance.

Fourth, and perhaps most significantly, works of interest to
oral literary historians are ones that can be read from the
perspective of audience analysis and audience reception. The
oral literary historian examines performance and contextual
factors in a work's creation. The term ''verbal performance''
refers to the influence on how and what is told to an anticipated audience, and how that anticipation shapes utterances
before they are spoken. These performance variables shape
any oral literary experience or speech act. In its most extreme circumstance—such as Ruth Finnegan's account of
African griots narrating a king's lineage—the makeup of

the immediate audience can determine the genealogy recounted.[2]

Literary historians have often accepted the challenge of interpreting the orality of written literary texts—as E. A. Bowden has in studies of the performed literature of Geoffrey Chaucer and Bob Dylan.[3] The oral literary historian takes for granted that texts generated orally are profoundly shaped by the presence (or absence) of an audience. Hence, a literary text may be studied from the perspective of the formulaic and archetypal patterns underlying extemporization and the use of traditional, tale- and motif-types that are embedded in contemporary narratives. Thus the oral literary historian profits from training in folkloristics, to guide in disentangling the traditional elements (motifs and tales) of accounts told as literal truth. Central to the interpretation of life stories, life histories, and family or historical saga is this role of performance, of storyfication.

The aesthetic formulae of story-telling inevitably influence information collected and published. The oral literary historian approaches a text rich with anecdote and colorful description; he or she may explore how the discourse rules of fiction have been evoked. In oral biography, for example, narrating one's life becomes a process of configuring actual events into a symbolic representation of personal mythology. The memoirist's words form a surface superstructure over embedded culture-specific and individual-specific hidden meanings; oral accounts mediate between life events and written texts. Thus the study of verbal performance as an art and profession is relevant to any study of oral literary history.[4]

The context, or audience environment, and the text's function provide crucial information to the oral literary historian. Not just the present audience and function, but the history of those audiences and those functions must be taken into account. Individuals create literary texts in an oral format for multiple reasons: catharsis, self-justification, self-aggrandizement, and self-enrichment are just a few of these.

Fifth, texts studied via oral literary history often show a

collaborative process fundamentally different from traditional written sources because of the interactive roles of interrogator and narrator. Collaborative process of interviewing shapes the finished product and its analysis. A text from centuries past can only be analyzed in its fixed form (although this recorded form was itself sometimes a result of "freezing" a fluid oral tradition, and is subject to revisions as the text is formulated into different editions). An oral text, on the other hand, is a joint creation of interviewer and interviewee, which invites examination of the dynamics of its creation. Thus the modern preoccupation of anthropologists, folklorists, linguists, and other social scientists to document their work reflexively is of particular importance to the oral literary historian. In cross-cultural (and cross-racial, cross-gender, and cross-class) situations, interviewers may accidentally reflect stereotypes that determine answers before questions are even asked.

A written document never talks back; and although the ability to cross-examine oral testimony is one of the great strengths of oral literary history, texts created collaboratively cannot be understood or analyzed in the same fashion as works of sole authorship. In analyzing a jointly created text, oral literary historians study the interviewer's models, methods, and intended audience; personal constraints (financial resources, writing and recording ability, and available time), demographic characteristics (including class, race, gender, and age), and the interviewer's relation to his or her subject (including distance, balance, and tone).[5]

From the narrator's perspective, the assessment of the interviewer's background, shrewdness, and experience may determine what information is revealed.

Oral Biography

Since the writings of Thucydides, oral historians have used interviews to amass biographical and historical information. In recent years this tendency has accelerated, with interviews of a biographical nature entering popular culture via radio, television, and film.

The oral biography, a nonfictional life narrative researched primarily through interviews, has helped to democratize history by incorporating perspectives of the nonliterate and of groups often excluded from the traditional historical canon. Anthropologists have turned to intensive oral interviewing to establish "life histories," narrated, culture-specific biographies of the unfamous. Sociologists have used orally gathered survey data to collect composite portraits of a people, as regional or national biographical overviews.

Oral biography possesses key advantages for contemporary research, as opposed to those works limited to written sources. Interview sessions expose new collections of documents, including letters and photographs; interviews cover a full range of sources, not just those from the period of public activity; the sources themselves are available for cross-examination; the testimonies are a rich depository of living language, with characteristically distinctive phrasings; and, finally, oral sources possess an authenticity based on the three-dimensional effects of collaboration among the biographer, the sources, and, occasionally, the subject himself.

These distinctive qualities of the orally sourced biography create works substantively and qualitatively different from those based exclusively on published records, letters, and journals. The oral biography is of necessity more collaborative and interactive. At times, the characters in literary works actually have a chance to talk back to an author's portraits, such as in the oral biography of Jack Kerouac, *Jack's Book.*[6] The biographer becomes, in effect, a fieldworker, and thus benefits from the growing literature on ethnographic interviewing and cross-cultural communication.

Among the most common literary formats for oral biography are: 1) the orally sourced biography, 2) the group memoir, and 3) the oral memoir. The orally sourced life relies primarily on oral sources' integrated written records; many contemporary biographies are of this sort. Here, oral sources are complementary, adding a dynamic and interactive dimension to static written and transactional records.

The second variety of oral biography, group interviews, are often presented in the form of edited and excerpted transcripts, such as in *Jack's Book,* Manso's *Mailer: His Life and Times,* or Spears and Cassidy's *Agee Remembered.* A subset of the group memoir is what might be called oral sociology, where the group's testimony concerns a single project, period, or place, as in Tony Parker's *Bird, Kansas.*[7]

The oral memoir, the as-told-to narrative of a life, is similarly based on interview transcripts and annotated through explanatory and documentary footnotes. The subject's own words are the foundation of the text, which may be enriched with documents and archival photos. This approach has had commercial success for movie actors and celebrities, e.g., Lee Iococca's memoirs, or the more scholarly *Copland: 1900–1942,* by Vivian Perlis.[8]

Each variety of oral biography has its strengths and drawbacks. The orally sourced book requires the interviewer-researcher to judge the reliability and validity of the narrators. The group memoir provides the freshness of multiple voices, rather than a single authorial conclusion. (Without annotation, however, the interviews may not add up to a satisfying whole.) The oral memoir can be a vivid recollection of historically significant events or a rambling, unedited collection of anecdote and one-sided vitriol, outside the historical or artistic context of the life's work.

Oral biographies can also be classified by historical period. In the *Times Literary Supplement,* Anthony Alpers, biographer of English writer Katherine Mansfield, proposed such a schema, starting with the historical biography, of figures deep in the historical past about whom present-day, firsthand accounts are impossible. For this type, oral testimony often amounts to the legends of folklore.[9]

A second type is the after-the-fact biography, five to fifty years after death, based on collections of documents, printed and private, plus oral accounts of friends, students, associates, family.

A third type—perhaps the most hazardous one, for a biographer—is the contemporary biography, written while the figure still lives. In this case, issues of authorization, libel/invasion of privacy, and access to private papers become critical.

Again, each type has distinct advantages and disadvantages for the oral biographer. The historical biographer relies on written accounts of the figure's contemporaries, who necessarily report only in the context of their times, and who cannot be cross-examined. A vast proportion of written source materials may have been lost over time, and there is scant assurance that what survives, even in the best of cases, is truly representative. The biographer's lack of firsthand impressions or conversations with his or her subject can impoverish characterization and narration. Furthermore, the subject may already be enveloped in layers of previous biography (or hagiography), which may take considerable courage to challenge or overturn.

In the after-the-fact biography, oral accounts enrich the subject's papers—which may be in the hands of those who zealously guard the deceased's memory, gatekeepers willing to suppress materials that contradict their memories or interests—more than a thorny problem. Oral testimony from these friends may be tainted by its unverifiable uniqueness.

The decision to organize a life according to these typologies of format or period depends on a biographer's subject and intent—whether writing to muckrake, psychoanalyze, defame, scandalize, canonize, or other, more admirable objectives. Whatever the intent in preparing and interpreting lives based on oral sources, oral biographers weigh their "texts" in an ethnographic context, exploring problems of evidence, memory, and verbal performance.

A central dilemma for oral biographers will be how the unique features of oral biography can be preserved (in particular, its collaborative, interactive narration; its vivid detail and lifelike phrases) while producing comprehensive, dependable records. No innovations in tape recording will yield this result; readers will have to rely on the discerning skills of a new generation of biographers, trained in oral, as well as written, historiography.

Notes: The Aldous Huxley Oral History Project

1. David Courtwright, Herman Joseph, and Don Des Jarlais, *Addicts Who Survived: An Oral History of Narcotic Use in America, 1923–1965* (Knoxville: University of Tennessee Press, 1989); Barry Gifford and Lawrence Lee, *Jack's Book: An Oral Biography of Jack Kerouac* (New York: St. Martin's Press, 1978). Tony Parker, *Bird, Kansas* (New York: Knopf, 1989); Vivian Perlis, *Copland: 1900–1942* (New York: St. Martin's Press, 1984).

Notes: Transcribing and Editing Oral History

1. The standard work on the subject is by Willa K. Baum, *Transcribing and Editing Oral History* (Nashville: American Association for State and Local History, 1977). Works on processing oral history by William Moss, Ronald Grele, and Cullom Davis et al. have also informed my procedures and the contents of the following essay.

2. Clifford Geertz, "The Impact of the Concept of Culture on the Concept of Man," in *Man Makes Sense*, ed. E. A. Hammel and W. S. Simmona (Boston: Little, Brown, 1965).

3. Willa K. Baum, *Transcribing and Editing Oral History* (Nashville: American Association for State and Local History, 1977), pp. 38–39.

4. The field of linguistic anthropology seems to hold the greatest promise of devising such a coding system for transcripts. Charles Briggs of Vassar College has presented a tentative system in *Learning to Ask* (New York: Cambridge University Press, 1989). See also Elizabeth Fine, *The Folklore Text* (Bloomington: Indiana University Press, 1984).

5. Noam Chomsky, *Syntactic Structures* (The Hague: Mouton, 1957).

6. Willa K. Baum, *Transcribing and Editing Oral History* (Nashville: American Association for State and Local History, 1977), p. 37.

7. For one description of the complex relationship between tran-

script and potential use, see Michael Frisch, "Preparing Interview Transcripts for Documentary Production," in *A Shared Authority: Essays on the Craft and Meaning of Oral and Public History* (Albany: SUNY Press, 1990); for a mass-broadcast use of oral history, see David Dunaway, "Radio and the Public Use of History," *The Public Historian*, vol. 6, no. 2 (Spring 1984), pp. 77–90.

Notes: Oral Literary History

1. For an overview of this theoretical linguistic approach, see Charles Briggs, *Competence in Performance* (Philadelphia: University of Pennsylvania Press, 1988).

2. Ruth Finnegan, "A Note on Oral Traditional Historical Evidence," in Dunaway and Baum, eds., *Oral History: An Interdisciplinary Anthology* (Nashville: American Association for State and Local History, 1984).

3. Betsy Bowden, *Performed Literature* (Bloomington: Indiana University Press, 1982), and *Chaucer Aloud* (Philadelphia: University of Pennsylvania Press, 1987).

4. For this sociolinguistic dimension to orality, see Richard Baumann, *Verbal Art as Performance* (Prospect Heights, Ill., Waveland Press, 1977), and *Story, Performance and Event: Contextual Studies in Oral Narrative* (Cambridge, Cambridge University Press, 1986).

5. See Sherna Gluck, "What's So Special About Women? Women's Oral History," *Frontiers: A Journal of Woman's Studies*, vol. 2 (Summer 1977), pp. 3–13.

6. Barry Gifford and Lawrence Lee, *Jack's Book: An Oral Biography of Jack Kerouac* (New York: St. Martin's Press, 1978).

7. Tony Parker, *Bird, Kansas* (New York: Knopf, 1989).

8. Vivian Perlis, *Copland: 1900–1942* (New York: St. Martin's Press, 1984).

9. Anthony Alpers, "Biography—The Scarlet Experiment," *Times Literary Supplement* (March 26, 1980), pp. 8–9.

INDEX

213